Grow It Yourself

Growing Veg for the 'Have a Go' Gardener

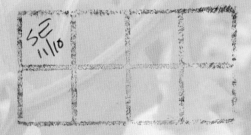

SE
11/10

Published by The Good Life Press Ltd., 2010

ISBN 978 1 90487 1477
A catalogue record for this book is available from the British Library.

Published by
The Good Life Press Ltd.
The Old Pigsties, Clifton Fields
Lytham Road
Preston PR4 0XG

www.goodlifepress.co.uk
www.homefarmer.co.uk

Set by The Good Life Press Ltd.
Printed and bound in the UK by Scotprint

Photograph Sources
Pages 4,5,7,8,16,19,21,25,26,32,43,47,48-49,50,51,58,63,72-73,74,75,76, 86,87,89,95,97,102,105,107(top),110 © Gail Harland, 119 R. Tott. Cover and all other photographs Fotolia

Index

Introduction

G rowing your own vegetables can be a uniquely satisfying experience. It enables you to save money on food bills and to ensure that the food you eat is fresh and full of vitamins rather than added chemicals. It helps to reduce the environmental impact of transporting food around the country too. The physical activity involved in working in the garden will promote fitness, whilst perhaps most important of all, being outdoors and in regular contact with nature can improve mental health and your quality of life. Many people are introduced to the pleasures of growing their own when they try growing a simple easy-to-grow plant such as the tomato and, having had some success, become enthused with the idea of growing crops.

The tomato is by far the most popular food crop with home gardeners in Britain and many other countries of the world. It is particularly successful when grown in greenhouses and polytunnels, but in good summers will also produce bumper crops outdoors. Cultivar selection is dominated by the traditional, medium-sized, round, red tomatoes such as 'Ailsa Craig', 'Alicante', 'Moneymaker', 'Shirley' and 'The Amateur'. Indeed, if you buy in plants from a garden centre selections such as these may be the only ones on offer, although some of the more popular small-fruited cultivars, for example 'Gardener's Delight' and 'Sungold', are also sometimes stocked.

However, if you are prepared to raise your own plants from seed a whole new world of exciting and varied forms of tomato opens up, ranging in size from no bigger than a pea to mammoths of 2kg (4lb) or more. Colours encompass shades of red, orange and yellow, but also more unusually white, green, plum-black and even stripy fruits. Even the shapes can vary tremendously from perfect spheres, beautiful heart-shaped cultivars ideal for a St Valentine's Day dinner, intriguing box-shaped forms such as 'Yellow Stuffer' which are virtually hollow and ideal for stuffing, to the frankly bizarre fruits of cultivars like 'Reisetomate' that look as though a whole bunch of cherry tomatoes have fused together. Many tomato plants are worth growing for their ornamental effect. Trailing forms of the small cherry type tomatoes like 'Trailing Tom Red' look beautiful cascading from a hanging basket and Angora types such as 'Elberta Girl' and 'Angora Super Sweet' have fuzzy stems and leaves that are densely covered in soft, silvery hairs.

Once you have experience of raising tomatoes from seed, the next step is to try some of the other varied fruit and vegetables that can be easily grown in the same manner as tomatoes. Plants such as peppers and

aubergines are usually said to need more heat than tomatoes, but whilst they may be more prolific in a hot summer or under the protection of a glasshouse, many cultivars will give a decent crop when grown in a simple tub on the patio. Indeed, they are often better than tomatoes for growing outdoors as, although they are in the same family, they are less likely to succumb to the fungal disease late blight.

There are cultivars of cucumbers suitable for both protected and outdoor cultivation. They can be surprisingly easy to grow and give great satisfaction when harvesting. As with tomatoes there is a wide choice of shapes and colours, from the traditional long green cucumbers to those the size and colour of a lemon and even plants such as the squirting cucumber that is grown purely for fun. Other salad crops such as lettuces, beetroot and radishes are as easy to grow in a hanging basket, patio tub or grow bag as in the traditional rows in the vegetable plot. It also makes them more difficult for slugs and other pests to reach, whilst remaining easily accessible for the cook who wants to nip out and harvest something for a quick lunch.

Tomatillos are close relatives of tomatoes, also known as husk tomatoes as the fruit is enclosed in a papery husk similar to that of the Cape gooseberry. They are very rarely found in supermarkets or greengrocers and yet are easy to grow, producing prolific crops from just a couple of plants. They are well worth trying as they give you the opportunity to prepare authentic Mexican green salsas as an accompaniment to bowls of chilli. The Cape gooseberry itself is usually just as productive in the home garden. Seed extracted from just one supermarket fruit will produce far more plants than are required to satisfy the average family.

The seed of many of these plants may not be as readily available as the standard varieties but there is an increasing number of specialist suppliers, many of whom are listed in the appendix, and you can even find a surprising selection of seed on internet auction sites. If you are interested in heritage cultivars then joining an organisation such as Garden Organic or the Cottage Garden Society may be the best way to obtain many seeds that are not found in commercial sources. Seed obtained from garden society seed lists has usually been harvested from private gardens where there is a chance of cross-pollination occurring between other cultivars in that or neighbouring gardens. You must therefore be prepared

Introduction

to accept that there will be some variability in seedlings raised from such sources.

Cultivars (simply a shortened way of saying cultivated varieties) include selections of wild plants such as the currant tomato, *Solanum pimpinellifolium*, as well as those that arose in cultivation. The choice of cultivars can actually be somewhat bewildering. There are thought to be over 5,000 cultivars of tomatoes alone, although despite legislation there are still many instances of the same plant being sold under a multitude of different names. Officially vegetable seeds can only be sold in countries of the European Union (EU) if the cultivar is registered with the EU's common catalogue of vegetable cultivars. Once a cultivar name is listed it cannot be changed, so translations of foreign names are not valid. Many good cultivars, particularly those raised in Eastern Europe, never become successful in the British or American markets simply because their names are considered unpronounceable.

Seed extracted from just one supermarket Cape gooseberry will produce far more plants than required to satisfy the average family.

When choosing what to grow, look out for those cultivars awarded an Award of Garden Merit (AGM) by the Royal Horticultural Society. The award is given to plants that show excellence for ordinary garden use and so plants with this award such as the heavy-cropping cucumber 'Marketmore' or red-leafed lettuce 'Pandero' should be productive and not susceptible to pests or diseases. In the United States the All-America Selections are those cultivars of flowers or vegetables declared the best after thorough testing by a network of independent judges. Recent winners of this award include the high-yielding pepper 'Holy Molé' in 2007 and the early, white-fruiting aubergine 'Gretel' in 2009.

The seed listed in catalogues is often described as either F1 hybrid or

Grow It Yourself

heirloom/heritage seed. A hybrid strictly speaking is the offspring of genetically different parents and so the word is one that could be applied to a fair proportion of all cultivars. F1 hybrids, however, are first generation plants produced by crossing selected pure-breeding parents to create uniform, vigorous offspring. F1 seed is more expensive to raise as the company producing it has to maintain two separate breeding lines and then cross them each year. Any seed saved from plants raised from this F1 seed does not come true in that the next generation of plants will probably not resemble their parents. This is a commercial advantage to the seed producer as it means that nobody outside the company can duplicate the F1 seed as they have sole possession of the parental stock, ensuring that customers return each year if they want more of that seed.

Plants from F1 seed are more popular with commercial growers as they usually exhibit greater uniformity and often show greater resistance to disease. The advantages, however, are not as great for crops like tomatoes which generally self-pollinate as for those which would readily cross-pollinate such as carrots. Many F1 hybrids have a relatively short commercial life of around five years before they are replaced by a newer cultivar, which can be frustrating if a favourite plant is no longer available. The degree to which future generations differ from the original F1 seed does vary greatly, so if you are growing a cultivar that does particularly well for you it may be worth experimenting by saving some seed yourself.

For commercial growers factors such as yield, disease resistance and the ability to survive packaging and transport may be the prime considerations when choosing cultivars. The home gardener on the other hand may consider such qualities of less importance than flavour. Of course taste is very much a subjective trait and can be influenced as much by growing conditions as by the actual cultivar chosen, however, the recent increase in popularity of many so-called heirloom fruits and vegetables has been fuelled in part by the perception that many old cultivars have a better flavour than modern crops.

There is no one universally accepted definition of what constitutes an heirloom cultivar, with some people arguing that only those plants that have been grown, selected and passed down by successive generations of a family or community qualify for the title, whereas others take the more pragmatic view that any treasured cultivar that is open-pollinated rather than hybrid-ised can be considered an heirloom. Open-pollinated seed is that which has been pollinated by natural means such as wind or insects. If the plants are isolated from other cultivars any seed produced from open pollinated cultivars  should produce plants that are true to type, although as bees can travel up to 5km (3miles) in search of food, so even if you are growing only one cultivar of a plant it may receive pollen from neighbouring plants. You can cover individual plants with insect proof cages made from canes and horticultural fleece, although plants such as tomatillos which are not self-fertile will then need to be hand pollinated. A more pragmatic approach is to accept that a certain level of genetic variability is inevitable.

There is a great nostalgic appeal to growing heirloom varieties and for many gardeners growing and saving seed from such plants is a way of connecting with their heritage or community. Of course you can develop your own strains of favourite crops by watching and selecting for particular characteristics that appeal to you. Alternatively you could actively breed your own plants by cross-pollinating two plants that show desirable traits and selecting the best offspring. By continually selecting and growing on only the best plants you can create your own heirloom plants which could be passed down to future generations of your family or even introduced commercially.

With such a huge range of plants available, growing plants from seed can easily become addictive and you may find that you do not have enough space to plant out everything you want to grow. Many plants can be grown successfully in containers on a patio or paved yard, but you can also find yourself speculatively eyeing the lawn or the children's play area and wondering whether to convert those into vegetable beds.

Grow It Yourself

With increasing concern about food bills, as well as the environmental aspects of food miles and the chemicals involved in commercial food production, it certainly makes sense to grow as much of your own food as possible. Growing food crops does not mean that you have to sacrifice having an ornamental garden as many fruits and vegetables are as attractive as more conventional flowers and can be grown cottage-style among the borders rather than in customary rows in a vegetable patch. They are actually often more successful grown in this manner as it makes them less obvious to pests than when vegetables are grown together in blocks. Cordon tomatoes can be trained against a sunny fence and plants such as climbing beans are ideal used as both ornamental and productive plants to scramble up a trellis or over garden arches.

Tip!

If it was the children's play area that disappeared in order to create space for edible plants, just remember to involve the children in cultivating the plants and hopefully by harvest time they will have forgiven you.

Converting areas of lawn into vegetable beds is certainly an option to consider. Lift the turf and stack it grass side down in an out of the way corner to allow it to mature into valuable loam. It is worth digging over the soil thoroughly before planting as it will usually contain pests such as leather jackets and wireworms which, deprived of their usual diet of grass roots, will attack your crops. Digging the soil exposes such pests to wild birds who will usually happily clear the ground for you. New beds can be made flat on the soil or you may prefer raised beds which can look very ornamental and certainly make gardening easier for those with restricted mobility. If it was the children's play area that disappeared in order to create space for edible plants, just remember to involve the children in cultivating the plants and hopefully by harvest time they will have forgiven you.

If you find that you really do not have sufficient land available for your requirements it is worth looking into the possibility of renting an allotment. Allotments are small areas of land rented to individuals, usually for the growing of food crops. The size of land varies but traditionally plots were ten rods, an ancient measurement roughly equivalent to 250 square metres. Allotments are usually owned by local government, although the Church of England owns a considerable amount of land and there are some privately owned sites. Allotment numbers peaked at around 1,400,000 during the Second World War as a result of the 'Dig for Victory' campaign but then fell to less than 300,000 plots by the 1980s. There is currently a great revival of interest in allotments with long waiting lists for sites. Some councils, corporations such as British Waterways and private organisations are creating new allotments on unused stretches of land to help meet the demand from people wanting to grow their own food. The National Trust announced in 2009 that it will create 1000 new allotments at around 40 different locations to help support the 'grow your own' revolution.

There is frequently a great camaraderie between people on the site and the sharing of knowledge and resources makes working an allotment quite a social activity. Walking around an allotment site can be fascinating as many plots have a great sense of individuality with people devoting much ingenuity and imagination to the raising of crops with limited resources. At some allotment sites the keeping of livestock such as chickens is permitted. Closely related to allotments are the community gardens seen particularly in the United States, Canada, Australia and New Zealand in which land is gardened by a group of people. They often result from local residents joining together to clear abandoned vacant lots and turning

them into gardens.

If taking on a new or overgrown plot, clearing the land to make it ready for crops can be quite intimidating. Start by cutting all the vegetation down to ground level with a strimmer, brush cutter, scythe or shears. The cut material can be composted except for very woody material and the perennial roots of plants like couch grass and ground elder which can easily regrow. The latter and any stems of ivy are best burnt or bagged into tough black plastic bags and left in an out-of-the-way corner to gradually rot down. Be careful before using this as compost as the stems of ivy can sometimes still be viable after a year. Either dig over the plot carefully removing any perennial roots, or wait for regrowth to appear and then spray with a non-residual weedkiller such as glycosphate. If you would prefer not to use weedkillers, cover the area with a thick light-resistant material for six months to a year to kill any remaining plants. Do not try to clear too much at once or you can quickly become disheartened. In the United Kingdom The National Society of Allotment and Leisure Gardeners is a useful source of advice.

The Vegetable Plot

From the floating gardens or chinampas of Montezuma's Aztec kingdom in Mexico to the Baroque fripperies of Louis XIV's potager at Versailles or the more prosaic neat rows of vegetables in an allotment garden, a kitchen garden can take virtually any form you wish. The key requirements are an open but not exposed site and preferably a fertile, well drained soil. The actual layout is very much a matter of personal taste. It is often more convenient for the gardener if food crops are grown together in their own beds, making the day-to-day cultivation straightforward. However, as already mentioned, growing crops in amongst flowers in a border in the cottage garden manner makes them less likely to be seen by pests than if grown together in blocks.

The use of raised beds is becoming increasingly popular. They improve soil drainage and so are particularly beneficial on heavy soils. They can be of any shape and size, although beds of not more than 1.2m (4ft) wide ensure that the centre of the bed can be easily reached so that all sowing, planting and general care can be done without walking on the soil, thus preserving the soil structure. Make sure that any timber used for the bed edgings

Grow It Yourself

Lilac as hedging looks and smells fabulous, but takes up space.

has been pressure treated with preservative or it will not last long when in contact with damp soil. A number of rectangular beds can be used for a vegetable garden or different shaped beds can be made into geometric patterns and filled with a combination of vegetables, herbs and flowers to make a French-style potager.

Site and Soil

Open sites not overshadowed by trees or buildings ensure that the plants receive plenty of light and do not have to compete with tree roots for water and nutrients. It is however important that the site is not too exposed, indeed providing shelter from the wind is vital as even light winds can decrease yields by at least a quarter, whilst on very exposed sites your crop may well be flattened. Hedges are usually the most effective form of windbreak as they allow the wind to filter through, avoiding the turbulence caused by a more solid structure.

The choice of plants for hedges is chiefly down to personal preference. A mixture of native species including plants such as hazel (*Corylus avellana*) and holly (*Ilex aquifolium*) is useful for encouraging wildlife. A formal evergreen hedge of yew (*Taxus baccata*) or other conifers provides a dense, year-round screen. The much-maligned Leyland cypress (x *Cupressocyparis leylandii*) is actually an ideal, fast-growing hedge and is particularly good at filtering out diesel particulates, an important consideration if your garden is close to a busy road or even in a rural site with a lot of tractor traffic. More informal flowering hedges using rugosa roses or lilacs (*Syringa vulgaris*) can look very attractive, although they usually take up more space. You could try a low productive hedge using plants such as redcurrants, gooseberries or, on acid soil, blueberries.

Hedges do have disadvantages in that they will take time to become established and require regular maintenance. They will also compete with the crop for soil, water and nutrients. Living willow screens are becoming very popular as they are relatively quick to produce by pushing willow rods into the ground and, when woven together well can look very attractive, although again they will require regular upkeep. Fences, woven hurdles or windbreak netting may be the simplest solution, although a temporary fast growing screen can be created from a row of sunflowers.

Tomatoes and other warm climate crops are best planted in the sunniest, most sheltered part of the garden. A position at the foot of a south-facing wall would be ideal. Shadier sites could be used for plants such as lettuces which can flag in hot weather. Many salad crops have a high water requirement and in warm summers will need frequent watering so try to ensure that they are planted close to a tap or water butt.

The ideal type of soil is that usually known as a 'medium loam' which is a fertile, moisture-retentive soil rich in organic matter and containing a balanced mixture of clay, sand and silt particles. A well structured soil will be free draining and well aerated and will support a healthy population of earthworms and beneficial microorganisms to break down organic matter, ensuring that most plants will grow well with little if any additional feeding.

Of course few of us are blessed with an ideal soil and instead we have to battle with heavy clay that is cold and sticky in winter and bakes to a rock-like texture in summer or a sandy soil that requires seemingly constant watering in hot weather or even sadly in some gardens a substrate that contains more builder's rubble than soil. Most soils can be greatly improved by the regular addition of organic matter such as home-made compost, well rotted animal manures, spent mushroom compost or leaf mould. Apply a thick layer, around 8-10cm (3-4in) deep to the soil surface each autumn, leaving the worms to work it into the soil. Areas of bare soil can be sown with a green manure such as mustard or Italian ryegrass. Once green manures get to around 20cm (8in) tall they are dug into the soil, releasing nutrients as they rot. Plants in the pea family, for example clover or agricultural lupins, have nitrogen-fixing bacteria in nodules on their roots and so make a particularly effective form of green manure. Using the marigold *Tagetes minuta* as a green manure is said to suppress eelworms in the soil.

Crop Rotation

If crops from the same family are grown year after year on a piece of land there may be a build up of soil-borne pests and diseases. Crop rotation is the practice of changing the position of annual crops in the garden each year to avoid such problems. Specific groups of vegetables are moved around in sequence so that they are not grown in the same area again for at least three years. Crop rotation also helps to make efficient use of soil nutrients as different crops have different nutrient requirements and alternating between deep-rooted and more fibrous rooted crops may improve soil structure. However, whilst crop rotation can be helpful, keeping to a strict rotation in a small garden may be impractical and to be completely effective the rotation would require a much longer timescale than the usual three to four years as some diseases such as club root, caused by the soil-borne slime mould *Plasmodiophora brassicae* which affects brassicas, can remain in the soil for twenty years or more.

If using a four yearly crop rotation, divide the vegetable garden into multiples of four. In the first area plant tomatoes and other members of the same family such as aubergines and potatoes with root crops such as carrots and beetroot. Follow on with members of the onion family and in the next year grow legumes such as peas and beans. Most vegetables in the legume family have nodules on their roots and can fix nitrogen in the soil, making it available for the next crop. It is therefore usual to follow legumes with nitrogen hungry brassicas such as cabbages and broccoli before returning to the tomato family and root crops again. Growing tomatoes in a rotation after cabbage or sweetcorn has been found to reduce the incidence of bacterial wilt. If you want to grow both tomatoes and potatoes, keep them apart as they share many of the same diseases; try planting a screen of tall marigolds between them.

FIRST PLOT	SECOND PLOT
Year 1	Year 1
Tomato family and root crops	Brassicas
Year 2	Year 2
Onion family	Tomato family
Year 3	Year 3
Legumes	Onion family
Year 4	Year 4
Brassicas	Legumes
THIRD PLOT	FOURTH PLOT
Year 1	Year 1
Legumes	Onion family
Year 2	Year 2
Brassicas	Legumes
Year 3	Year 3
Tomato family	Brassicas
Year 4	Year 4
Onion family	Tomato family

Keeping the soil fallow, that is not growing anything on it for a season, can be helpful in reducing populations of some soil borne pests such as nematodes as they will die out through lack of food. Digging the soil over will help as the nematodes will be exposed to the drying effect of the sun and wild birds can also then more easily find many other grubs.

Grow It Yourself

Sowing and Planting

Sow hardy vegetables outside in late winter or early spring when soil temperatures reach around 6°C (43°F). The traditional way to tell if temperatures were suitable was to drop your trousers and sit on the ground; if you could sit without undue discomfort then the seeds could go in. Using a thermometer is probably a more practical method and is certainly less likely to cause consternation amongst your neighbours! The soil can be warmed for earlier sowing by covering it with cloches or black plastic sheeting.

Tomatoes, aubergines, peppers and many of the related crops will benefit from being started off under cover. Even hardy crops can be started indoors and this has several advantages. It is helpful in areas with short seasons, enabling plants to get a head start before conditions outside are suitable. Temperatures are more easily controlled under cover and so germination may be more even and seedlings raised indoors are less likely to be attacked by pests. Starting seeds too early can, however, lead to plants becoming straggly due to insufficient light levels, although those gently stroked for about a minute each day (a technique that delights in the name of thigmomorphogenesis) will develop a more robust habit.

Seed is commonly sown in pots or seed trays and then pricked out when the seedlings have two or three small leaves. Alternatively individual modules can be used which produce high quality plants as they do not have to compete with their neighbours and suffer minimal root disturbance when potted on or planted out. When sowing it is best to use a compost specifically designed for seeds because a final potting mix may have too high a level of nutrients, inhibiting germination.

Plants started off in a protected environment will need a transition period to get them used to the conditions outside. Hardening off is the process of gradually letting young plants adapt to the sunlight, wind and fluctuating temperatures outdoors. Start by putting plants outside for an hour or so one day, working up to 5 or 6 hours over a period of a week. Try to avoid putting them in full sun or windy situations during this time. If you have a cold frame or glass cloche, this can be a useful halfway stage between the heated environment and outdoors. Alternatively cover

Tomatoes, aubergines, peppers and many of the related crops will benefit from being started off under cover. Here aubergine 'Black Stem' thrives in the greenhouse.

young plants with a layer of horticultural fleece until they are established, providing protection against many pests as well as the weather.

Some growers like to soak the roots with water or a diluted solution of seaweed fertilizer a couple of hours before transplanting. Making sure that the rootball is moist but not soggy enables it to slip out of the pot more easily. Check that the plants have a good healthy root system first by tipping one out of its pot. Be careful not to damage the roots as this can set the plant back. Transplanting on an overcast, still day will reduce stress from sun and wind. In areas where cutworms are a problem make newspaper or cardboard collars to slip around the base of the stem of the young plant to protect it until it is robust enough to resist attack.

Tip!

Some growers like to soak the roots with water or a diluted solution of seaweed fertilizer a couple of hours before transplanting. Making sure that the rootball is moist but not soggy enables it to slip out of the pot more easily.

Grow It Yourself

Routine Cultivation

Strongly growing, healthy plants are better able to cope with pests and diseases, so the use of good cultivation techniques is an important part of disease prevention. Provide an appropriate soil or compost with a good supply of organic matter, avoiding compacted, poorly drained soil. Water regularly, especially in dry weather. It is better to give a thorough watering each time rather than more frequent light watering in order to encourage the plants to root deeply into the soil. The best time of day to water is in the early morning before the sun gets hot enough to evaporate it off. Watering in the evening is a sure way of encouraging every slug and snail in the area to come and feast on your plants.

Having a water butt means that you can collect the rainwater running off the roof of your home, which is a valuable free resource. Rainwater is generally soft and free of chemical additives making it ideal for lime-intolerant plants such as blueberries and cranberries in areas where the tap water is hard. Water collected from roofs will however be affected by the material used on the roof surface. Galvanised metal roofs for example can contribute significant concentrations of zinc and water run-off from concrete tiles can be surprisingly alkaline. The water from a glasshouse roof is likely to be the purest. Always have a lid on your water butt to prevent debris entering and make sure that it is childproof if children use the garden. You can get low pressure watering kits or pumps which can produce mains like pressure from your water butt. These can be used even if there is a hosepipe ban in your area.

The flavour of many vegetables such as tomatoes is generally considered to be better if they have not been overwatered and equally, being too generous with fertilisers can result in lush growth but a reduction in flavour. Taste is very subjective so it is difficult to give hard and fast rules but you may find it interesting to compare results from some plants which have been grown hard with those which have been given regular additional fertiliser. There is a wide range of different commercial plant fertilisers, both organic and chemically based. Choose one specifically designed for the crops you are growing; do not use a lawn feed for tomatoes for example as lawn feeds have a high nitrogen content to encourage lush growth whereas tomatoes require a higher potassium feed. Many gardeners make their own fertiliser by rotting down comfrey leaves, nettles or other leafy plants and using the resulting dark liquid.

Mulching will help to reduce water evaporation from the soil and should keep weeds down. Organic mulches such as composted bark or well rotted garden compost help to improve soil structure as they are incorporated by worms. Black plastic or woven mulch mattings are excellent for weed control and can also increase springtime soil temperatures by as much

Marigolds are thought to be good at repelling whitefly. Here they are planted alongside tomatillos.

as 7 degrees which is useful for crops such as aubergines and peppers. In hot summers, however, they can contribute to excessive soil temperatures. Whilst the woven membranes are porous to water, in practice you usually find the water runs off rather than soaks through, so you will need to check that enough water is getting to your plants. Plants with a black plastic mulch will require especially careful watering. Research indicates that red plastic mulches reflect intensified red light to young plants, increasing their ability to photosynthesize and may result in increased cropping in tomatoes and strawberries. Some people may be unhappy about the aesthetics of red plastic mulches in a garden situation but they could be worth experimenting with.

Companion planting is the practice of growing plants that may have a beneficial effect on their neighbours. Such plants may be those which encourage pollinating insects such as lavenders and borage or alternatively those that repel pests. Native Americans traditionally grew 'three sister' vegetables together for their mutual benefit. Corn plants were used as supports for climbing beans which have nitrogen-fixing bacteria in their root nodules, with squashes covering the ground between them and suppressing weeds with their large leaves. Marigolds, particularly the French marigold *Tagetes patula*, are thought to be particularly good at repelling whitefly and even nematodes present in the soil. They are long-flowering plants and, like nasturtiums (*Tropaeolum majus*), will also attract many pollinators.

Bees are particularly useful as not only will they pollinate your crop but also studies have shown that caterpillars will stop moving or drop off the plant they are feeding on when stressed by buzzing bees. In an experiment reported in the journal Current Biology on sweet peppers, those plants kept in tents with bees suffered up to 70 percent less leaf damage than those which were unprotected, presumably because caterpillars, like many humans, cannot distinguish between bees and predatory wasps. Growing a mixture of flowering plants amongst your vegetable crops in potager fashion may therefore have unexpected benefits as well as looking attractive.

Tip!

Remember the old saying 'One year's seeding makes seven year's weeding' and pull all weeds before they set.

Maintain good plant hygiene by removing and burning any infected plant material. Do not put such material on a compost heap as any pathogens may remain alive and would be a source of infection to any subsequent crops grown in the compost. Eradicate any weeds which would compete with the crop for water and nutrients and may harbour disease organisms. The simplest way to remove weeds is to run a hoe over the bed or between rows. Choose a dry, breezy day to ensure the weeds die rather than just reroot as soon as your back is turned. More established weeds can be removed by hand. Make sure that you pull annual weeds before they set seed, remembering the old saying 'One year's seeding makes seven year's weeding'. Flame guns can be used to scorch off weeds growing between paving. Use them when the foliage is dry and allow sufficient burn time to kill the roots of deep-rooted weeds.

Allow plenty of space between plants to encourage air circulation and reduce the spread of any pests or diseases. Try to keep foliage dry to minimise fungal infections. Crops prone to fungal diseases should be planted where they will get the morning sun which helps to dry any dew from the leaves. Avoid overhead watering, particularly late in the day.

Slugs and snails often cause the most problems, particularly with young seedlings. Garden slugs (*Arion hortensis* Agg.) will even burrow into the soil to depths of 1m (3ft), so nothing is really safe from them. Softhearted gardeners who relocate such pests away from their garden should be aware that many molluscs show homing pigeon tendencies. Try repelling surface-feeding slugs and snails with barriers of grit, ashes or broken eggshells spread in a circle around young seedlings. Such barriers will need regular topping up after disturbance by rain or wind. Some people use spent coffee grounds as caffeine has been shown to be toxic to slugs. However, regulations made under the Food and Environment Protection Act 1986 make it illegal to use any chemical as a pesticide in Britain unless it has been approved for that purpose, which applies to even something as widely used as coffee. Interestingly, although it is illegal to use coffee as a pesticide, adding the grounds to your compost heap or garden as a soil improver is fine. The Sunset magazine in the United States sent a batch of Starbucks' used coffee grounds, which the company gives away freely to anyone wanting them, to a soil laboratory for analysis. They found that the grounds are slightly acidic and provide generous amounts of phosphorus, potassium, magnesium, and copper. They also release nitrogen into the soil as they degrade.

Copper tapes and copper impregnated mats are also available to deter slugs. The use of slug pellets containing metaldehyde is still thought to be the most effective method of killing slugs, but they must be used with care to prevent pets or wildlife consuming them. In 1998 pesticides were implicated in 90 poisoning incidents of dogs and cats of which 23 incidences involved molluscicides. Traps such as halves of grapefruit are commonly used, enabling the slugs to be collected and disposed of. There is a biological control available to control slugs in the ground. The nematode *Phasmarhabditis hermaphrodita* is a microscopic eelworm which enters the bodies of slugs, infecting them with a bacterial disease. The nematodes are sold in some garden centres or can be obtained by mail order. They are watered into the soil and require moist soils and a minimum temperature of 5°C (41°F).

Encourage natural predators such as wild birds, hedgehogs and frogs and toads into the garden as they can be very beneficial allies in the war against pests. Trees and shrubs provide shelter and cover from predators. Having a small pond in the garden will encourage frogs and toads, which are active predators of slugs and snails. Supply a variety of nestboxes to encourage breeding birds to use the garden as even small birds can consume large quantities of aphids and other pests when rearing a family. Providing water and supplementary feeding will help birds through hard winters.

Domestic ducks are very effective predators of slugs and smaller snails, but sometimes young ducks have to be shown that snails are good to eat. You may need to smash one or two to demonstrate that there is meat inside. Remember that if free range, ducks may tend to munch on your vegetable crops too. Sadly chickens are not so good at keeping slug numbers down as they do not seem to like their beaks getting slimy. They will, however, relish many other pests including vine weevils and their larvae and grubs such as leather jackets and cutworms.

Vegetables Under Cover

A windowsill is fine for starting off the seeds of more tender plants, but if seed sowing becomes compulsive you may find it useful to have a cold frame or greenhouse to take the excess. Having facilities for some form of protected cropping gives you far more flexibility in what you can grow and allows you to extend the growing season so that you will be able to harvest something for the kitchen all year round. Growing crops such as tomatoes under cover gives them much greater protection from diseases such as late blight, although some pests, for example white fly and red spider mite, also appreciate the warmer conditions and can cause problems.

A cold frame is any low enclosure used to provide a protected micro-climate for plants. They usually have a glass or poly-carbonate lid and may also have glass sides, although they are traditionally made from a wooden framed box with an old window as a lid. The roof should be sloped towards the sun to capture more light and to allow the rain to run off. Hinged tops can be wedged open on sunny days to prevent plants overheating, but a sliding lid will be less vulnerable

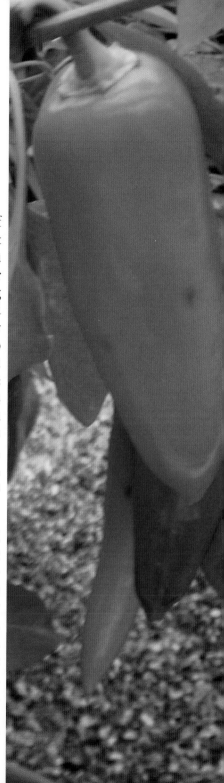

to sudden gusts of wind. Cloches are generally smaller than cold frames and can be used to protect individual plants. The beautiful glass bell-jar style cloches beloved of Victorian gardeners are now becoming available as reasonably priced reproductions. The term cloche is also applied to constructions made by stretching plastic film or horticultural fleece over wire hoops. These are ideal for growing salad crops such as lettuces and radicchio.

Permanently positioned cold frames should be on soil with a thoroughly prepared base of drainage material such as coarse gravel topped with a layer of 15cm (6in) or more of compost or good garden soil. Make sure that the frame is positioned where it will receive plenty of light in the winter and early spring months. Lightweight frames can be moved around the garden as required but may need ground anchors to ensure that they do not blow over on exposed sites.

Cold frames and cloches are widely used when germinating seedlings or for hardening off young plants in springtime. Small individual cloches made from cut-off plastic bottles or jam jars are useful for protecting vulnerable plants such as newly planted seedlings. Low growing crops

such as lettuces can also be grown directly in the cold frame if required to produce an earlier crop than those grown without protection.

Greenhouses and polytunnels are ideal for growing taller crops such as cordon tomatoes and aubergines and for overwintering tree tomatoes and other tender plants. They also make a more pleasant working environment for the gardener in wet or windy weather. Glass is an excellent transmitter of light and also retains heat well, so creating an ideal growing environment for plants. A greenhouse though is expensive and as a considerable investment for the garden, should be used to its fullest potential. Polytunnels are often considered to be a poor relation of the glasshouse but whilst even their most devoted users would not claim they are pretty, they can be an extremely cost-effective alternative with modern durable covers able to last at least five years. They are more difficult to ventilate than glasshouses and more vulnerable to damage by stray footballs etc. as once the polythene is torn no amount of taping and fixing will hold the structure together for long, whereas it is relatively easy to replace a single pane in a glasshouse.

Within the greenhouse or polytunnel structure plants can be grown either within soil beds or in containers. Growing within the bed gives crops a greater depth for root development which can reduce the need for watering and additional fertilisers. However, when crops are grown continuously in the same soil a build-up of serious pests and diseases can develop. Where soil-borne diseases occur replacement of the soil is sometimes recommended but this is a laborious process. There is a form of Caliente mustard used as a green manure which has been bred to have soil fumigant properties. Seed of this crop is sown in the autumn and the young plants dug or rotavated into the soil in the spring then sealed under black polythene for two weeks. In contact with moist soil the plants break down releasing the biologically active compound isothio-cyanate (naturally present in brassica plants) that will help to suppress nematodes and diseases such as root rot and Verticillium wilt. After two weeks the polythene is removed and the soil raked over before planting the next crop.

The greenhouse really comes into its own in the colder months of the year, allowing you to extend the season during which you can grow plants and enables you to grow more exotic crops such as tree tomatoes which would be killed by winter temperatures outside in the garden. The temperature at which you keep your greenhouse will depend on what crops you want to grow. An unheated greenhouse will provide suffi-cient protection to grow summer crops and to overwinter slightly tender plants. However, in order to keep out frost you will need a heater of some kind. An electric heater with a thermostat is the most efficient but without a source of power, gas or paraffin heaters may be used, although it is important to ensure that the greenhouse is well ventilated to prevent water vapour and fumes building up.

Adding a layer of bubblewrap polythene to the inside of the glass can help to insulate the greenhouse and keep heating costs down in the winter. Alternatively you could use a layer of horticultural fleece over tender plants during cold spells. Damp greenhouses can cause many problems, particularly over winter as they will encourage moulds and rots to affect the plants. Try and deal with any leaks promptly and ventilate the green-house freely on sunny days to help expel surplus moisture. Check plants regularly and remove any dying leaves or other plant debris which could act as a starting point for moulds.

The time when winter turns to spring is generally the busiest time in the glasshouse so take advantage of the quieter winter months to keep up with glasshouse maintenance. Keeping the glass clean is important to allow good light penetration, promoting healthy plant growth and reducing problems with pests and diseases. Choose a dry, breezy day for cleaning the glass so that you can have doors and ventilators open to assist with drying the glasshouse off afterwards. Scrub the glass

Tip!

Adding a layer of bubblewrap polythene to the inside of the glass can help to insulate the greenhouse and keep heating costs down in the winter.

inside and out with a soft brush or sponge. Clear any moss and algae growth from cracks between the glass panes using something like a plastic plant label or with careful use of a jet wash.

Wipe down all benching and pots, checking under the rims of pots where small snails and mealy bugs like to lurk. Ideally capillary matting would be replaced each year, but you can soak it in a suitable outdoor cleaning agent then hang it over a fence to dry. Horticultural fleece can be washed on a gentle setting in an automatic washing machine, but that may get you in trouble with whoever is in charge of the household laundry.

In the summer months ventilation will be particularly important to keep plants from overheating. Few greenhouses are supplied with sufficient vents as standard. Louvre ventilators can be fitted to the sides of the greenhouse to improve airflow through the structure. Hinged vents on the roof should open wide to an angle of around 45°. Make sure that they are securely fixed so that they will not be damaged by strong gusts of wind. Doors can be kept open in summer to increase ventilation but you may need to fix netting over the doorway to exclude pests. Shading helps control glasshouse temperatures in summer and protects crops such as tomatoes from sun scorch. Shading washes applied to the outside of the glass are the simplest and usually most effective way of reducing heat levels whilst allowing sufficient light for plant growth. In hot weather 'damp down' the greenhouse by watering the soil and paths to increase the humidity and lower temperatures which will discourage pests such as red spider mite. Try to avoid wetting plant foliage as this can make them more susceptible to fungal attacks.

Control any insect pests such as thrips and whitefly as these can act as vectors for viruses. If you do not like to use pesticides you could try growing a selection of carnivorous plants alongside your crops. Sundews such as *Drosera aliciae* and *D. capensis* have leaves covered in hairs which are each tipped with a glistening drop of glue. Pests get stuck to the glue and in some species the leaf folds around the struggling insect. The unicorn plant *Proboscidea louisianica* is not actually carnivorous but does have leaves liberally covered in glandular hairs, so they are almost as sticky as flypaper and indeed, in Central and South-Eastern America are used to de-louse chickens. Such plants will not, of course, be sufficient to deal with a major pest outbreak but as with commercially available sticky yellow traps, they can act as a useful indicator of the presence of pests such as whitefly.

Tip!

If you do not like to use pesticides you could try growing a selection of carnivorous plants alongside your crops. Sundews such as Drosera aliciae and D. capensis have leaves covered in hairs which are each tipped with a glistening drop of glue.

In a greenhouse the use of biological controls can be very helpful to combat pests such as aphids, whitefly, thrips and red spider mite. Biological control is simply a term used to describe the method of controlling pests that relies on natural mechanisms such as predation by insects or birds or parasitism by species whose immature stage develops within an insect host, ultimately killing the host. Do everything you can to encourage normal garden predators such as ladybirds and the larvae of hoverflies and lacewings, which can eat large numbers of aphids. If you need more help in combating pests, particular biological controls are available commercially for many greenhouse pest species. They can usually be bought from garden centres or mail order suppliers.

Thrips, sometimes known as thunder flies, can be controlled by the tiny mites *Amblyseius cucumeris* that crawl around on leaves and within flower buds looking for the thrips larvae. They can be used in greenhouses but also in the garden outside in the summer months in sheltered areas. They need to be kept at a temperature of at least 15°C to be most effective. You can buy the mites either loose in a tub or as a pack of slow-release sachets which you can hang up among the plants. *Encarsia formosa* are tiny parasitic wasps which provide control of greenhouse whitefly

(*Trialeurodes vaporariorum*). Each female wasp lays 100-200 eggs inside the whitefly nymphs. The wasp larvae hatch and develop inside the whitefly, killing them. *Encarsia formosa* are sold on small card squares that contain parasitized whitefly scale and more than 1,000 *Encarsia*.

The glasshouse red spider mite *Tetranychus urticae* is particularly problematic indoors as it breeds rapidly in warm, dry conditions and many strains are resistant to insecticides. It sucks the sap of a wide range of plants, resulting in a fine, pale mottling developing on the upper leaf surface. In heavy infestations silk webbing can be seen on the plants and the leaves will lose their green colour and dry up. Heavily infested plants are severely weakened and may die. Infestations can be controlled using the predatory mite *Phytoseiulus persimilis*. It needs good light and daytime temperatures of 21°C (70°F) or more, so is usually just used in the summer months.

Vine weevil larvae can be a particular problem for any plants overwintering in the polytunnel as they hide unseen in the compost eating the roots of the plants. You may not realise that they are there until a plant starts to look sick. Any plant wilting when the compost is moist should be tipped from the pot to check if these pests are eating the roots. The larvae are small white grubs with brown heads. They can be controlled using *Steinenema kraussei*, which are microscopic nematode worms that you water into the compost.

In protected environments such as cold frames and polytunnels crops will grow at a considerably faster rate and mature much earlier than outdoor crops. Growing some plants inside and some outdoors will ensure that you can harvest over an extended period of time. Otherwise it is a good idea to sow quick maturing crops little and often to ensure that you have a constant supply for the kitchen.

The Vegetable Plot

Tip!

Growing some plants inside and some outdoors will ensure that you can harvest over an extended period of time. Otherwise it is a good idea to sow quick maturing crops little and often to ensure that you have a constant supply for the kitchen.

Small Scale Crop Production

It is perfectly possible to grow a wide range of edible crops in the smallest of gardens or even if you have no garden at all. Miniature tomatoes such as 'Micro-Tom', many peppers and cut-and-come-again salad leaves will certainly grow well in pots on the kitchen windowsill. The shorter cultivars of aubergines eg. 'Baby Rosanna' and compact, quick-maturing salad vegetables such as beetroot, lettuces and radishes are easy to raise in window boxes and trailing forms of tomatoes look extremely ornamental cascading from a hanging basket. For gardeners with the use of a balcony, patio or any paved area there are endless possibilities for growing crops in containers. Troughs filled with different cultivars of ruby chard, smaller fruiting sweet peppers and a scatter of nasturtiums are as attractive as any orna-mental plantings and yet will also provide useful crops for the kitchen.

Small raised beds are ideal for tending by the elderly or infirm and even children will enjoy growing vegetables if they have a small bed dedicated to their own use. Beds made up to 1.2m (4ft) wide make it easy to reach the plants from both sides. Beds can be created from gravel boarding with wooden pegs to support the corners or raised bed kits can easily be bought at garden centres, although these are obviously more expensive than making your own.

The kinds of containers used to grow plants are really limited only by your imagination. The more conventional may stick with flowerpots, barrels and commercial grow bags, however virtually anything can be pressed into service, from cracked buckets, watering cans, wooden wine boxes and old sinks to the children's cast-off Wellington boots, which they will enjoy planting up with cherry tomatoes or alpine strawberries. Ordinary hanging baskets can be planted up or you could use unwanted colanders or old-fashioned kettles in a quirky kitchen garden.

Generally speaking the larger the container the better as a greater volume of compost available will provide the plants with more reserves of water and nutrients, and so you will have to water and feed less frequently. Good drainage is important as most vegetables are intolerant of soggy soils which will lead to rapid root death. If it is difficult to make drainage holes in your chosen container, fill the base with crocks or stones before adding compost and be very careful not to overwater. As a general rule however it is not necessary to put crocks in the bottom of pots and studies have shown that this can actually hinder drainage by impeding the capillary flow of water.

Deep containers which allow for a greater root depth tend to give the best results. Plants such as tomatoes and aubergines grow particularly well in 'long tom' type pots or deep florists' buckets. Florists' buckets are often sold off cheaply by supermarkets or florists' shops, especially in the periods after particularly busy times such as Mothers' Day and Easter. Happily these times usually coincide well with planting up your tender vegetables. Drill holes in the base of the buckets for drainage. Ordinary buckets can of course be used too and have the advantage that the handle makes them easier to move around as required.

When it comes to choosing which crops to grow in your container, shallow containers are really only suitable for shallow rooting plants such as lettuces, cornsalad, radishes and spring onions. Containers of 20cm (8in) or more deep can be used to grow a much greater range including carrots, chilli peppers and tomatoes such as 'Balconi Red', 'Gartenperle' and 'Tumbler'. Large tubs can be home to any of the plants featured in the following pages, even the more vigorous tomatoes and tomatillos.

Grow It Yourself

Grow compact cultivars of standard vegetables, many of which are marketed as 'mini vegetables'. Examples include the miniature pumpkin 'Baby Bear', cauliflower 'Igloo', the dwarf pea 'Tom Thumb' and lettuces 'Little Gem' and 'Mini Green'. Unfortunately the mini sweetcorn cultivars are not a good use of space as the plants themselves are usually just as big as normal sweetcorn

Here grow bags have been turned sideways to provide extra root space.

cultivars and they tend to only produce a handful of tiny cobs. Mini courgettes are easily obtained simply by harvesting any cultivar when the fruits are just fingerlength. For genuinely small plants you want a compact variety such as 'Defender' or the spineless plant 'Midnight'. Ordinary cultivars of carrots and beetroot will give a good crop of mini roots when spaced closely together and can be grown perfectly happily in a bucket.

Use good quality potting composts which should be well aerated. Buying very cheap composts from the DIY store often turns out to be a false economy, although you can mix them with garden compost and added perlite or grit to improve drainage. Loam-based John Innes type composts tend to be the most stable for long-term crops and are heavier, which can be a factor to consider if you want to plant top-heavy plants in an exposed site. If you are planting on a balcony or roof garden remember that the weight aspect may be more critical. If ordinary garden soil is used, mix it with an equal volume of well rotted compost or composted bark to lighten it so that it does not become compacted with frequent watering. Garden compost that is full of weed seeds can be used in the bottom half of a deep container so long as a sterile compost is used on top. Water absorbent granules can be incorporated in the compost to improve water retention.

Small Scale Crop Production

Most crops will do best in a sunny, sheltered position, particularly early in the season. Tender fruiting crops such as tomatoes, cucumbers and aubergines will benefit from the warmth of a sunny wall. Salad and leafy vegetables will crop well in semi-shade. One of the advantages of growing vegetables in containers is that you can move the containers around to follow the sun if no one spot in your patio or garden is suitable. In hot summers it may be better to move pots to a semi-shaded spot to reduce sun scorch and to cut down on the amount of watering that you need to do.

Containers will dry out rapidly in hot and windy weather and you may find that even in rainy conditions you have to keep watering as plants with a lot of foliage can divert the raindrops away from the compost. Terracotta pots may look attractive but they do tend to dry out quickly. If this is a problem you can line them with perforated plastic bags. The best tool to use to see if plants need watering is the gardener's index finger: water when the compost feels dry. Make sure that you water thoroughly rather than just giving pots a flick with the hosepipe. If the compost has been allowed to dry out, stand the pot in a larger container of water if practical in order to allow it to get thoroughly wet again. To conserve moisture mulch the compost with a 5cm (2in) layer of gravel or organic matter. In hot summers or if you are going to be away, it may be worth installing a drip irrigation system. Simple systems are relatively inexpensive or you can install a sophisticated computer controlled watering system.

Hanging baskets can dry out particularly quickly and may need watering several times a day. Lining the basket with a perforated plastic liner or a plastic plant saucer helps to reduce evaporation or you can buy baskets with an integral water reservoir. Try putting a handful of ice cubes into the basket each morning so that they can melt gradually and release water into the basket. A variation on the hanging basket is the upside down planter usually marketed for growing cherry tomatoes but equally suitable for peppers, strawberries and herbs. Made of woven polyethylene fibres, these can be filled with compost and a plant inserted through a reinforced opening in the bottom. They have a self-watering reservoir at the top which is filled with water. A capillary strip ensures that the plant can draw on water as required and the reservoir will last a mature plant several days, even in hot weather.

Grow It Yourself

Tip!

Buying very cheap composts from the DIY store often turns out to be a false economy, although you can mix them with garden compost and added perlite or grit to improve drainage.

Container-grown vegetables may need more additional fertilisers than those grown in the ground due to the extra watering that they receive. Nutrients will be washed away quicker in a container than in the ground. Feed regularly using an appropriate organic or artificial fertilizer. Fruiting crops such as peppers, tomatoes and aubergines are best fed with a high potash tomato-type feed. Feed either with a liquid feed a couple of times a week or for greater ease use a slow release fertiliser added to the potting compost.

Containers and grow bags are often used in protected cropping, especially if the soil is infected with soil-borne disease. Grow bags are sealed plastic bags filled with a proprietary growing medium and can be peat based or use a peat substitute. You can use ordinary bags of compost as an alternative. Most of the nutrients in the growing medium will be used up during the year so fresh bags are bought each year, although sometimes they may be used for a subsequent successful crop of strawberries. The old compost can be used as a soil improver in the garden. Standard grow bags generally contain just 35 litres of compost and can be difficult to use for crops such as tomatoes as there is little depth for rooting and so they are prone to drying out rapidly. Bigger bags containing twice as much compost are becoming more widely available. They are usually marketed as tomato or salad planters and do make watering easier and give higher yields.

As an alternative you can try ring culture which involves putting three bottomless pots on top of the growbag. Using the pots as a template, cut rings into the surface of the bag and twist the pot into the compost below. Deep plant tomato plants into the pots and fill with compost, leaving just a couple of centimetres at the top to allow for watering. Tomato plants will put roots out from the stem where it is surrounded by compost, giving the plants more stability and a greatly increased ability to absorb water and nutrients.

Small Scale Crop Production

Tough woven polyethylene bags are being widely marketed for growing potatoes on patios. The bags usually have a 50 litre (13 gallon) capacity and can be used to grow four or five seed potatoes or other root crops such as carrots, parsnips or Jerusalem artichokes. Rectangular bags in various sizes are also becoming more available and are easy to use for a wide range of crops. They usually have handles on the side to make them easy to move. They are, it must be said, not the most attractive of containers and so for prime positions on the patio woven willow surrounds can be bought for them which are far more pleasing to look at.

To maximise the production obtained from your containers, sow a succession of crops in modules in order to have a constant supply of young plants coming on to replace the ones that you harvest. Intercropping slow growing crops like leeks with fast growers such as radishes and lettuces makes a particularly efficient use of space. You do need to make sure that the short-term crop is not shaded out before it is mature.

Pests and other problems will occur from time to time. Growing plants in hanging baskets keeps all but the most acrobatic of slugs and snails at bay, but it is surprising how acrobatic they can be at times. You can defend plants in pots with strips of copper tape around the rim of the pot, but slugs will cheerfully use any trailing foliage as a bridge to cross the copper. There are also boards available to sit your pots on; these are impregnated with salt and sulphates to repel molluscs. Flying pests of course can visit even your hanging baskets. Constant vigilance and a lack of squeamishness will enable you to squash any aphids or caterpillars before they do too much damage. Try planting French marigolds in with your crops to attract beneficial pollinating insects and ward off whitefly.

You may find, however, that plants grown in small raised beds or containers are easier to care for than those in the open garden. When closely spaced together they quickly cover the available ground and so can prevent weed seeds from germinating. They are also easy to cover with fine netting or horticultural fleece, enabling them to be protected from carrot or cabbage root flies, and attack by caterpillars or pigeons.

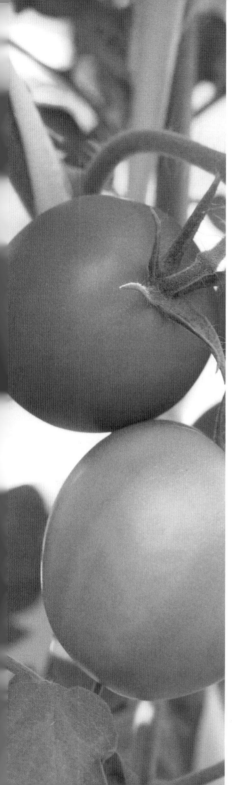

Tomatoes

From the ancient Aztecs to Mrs Beeton and many of our top modern chefs, the tomato has long been considered an important culinary item. Tomatoes originated in the coastal highlands of western South America and are still found wild today in Peru, Ecuador and northern Chile and also in the Galapagos Islands where they are thought to have been transported in the stomachs of turtles. They were grown by the Mayan and other peoples of Central America and were appreciated by the Aztecs from whom we get the word tomato. The Aztecs also used the tomatillo, *Physalis ixocarpa*, a native of the Mexican highlands, which they called tomatl. They named the tomato xitomatl (large tomatl) but when the Spanish introduced the tomato to Europe in the sixteenth century they just used the tomatl word.

Recent work by Peralta, Knapp and Spooner indicates that there are some 15 wild species of tomatoes within the genus *Solanum* that also includes related plants such as the potato, *Solanum tuberosum*, the aubergine, *S. melongena* and perhaps more worryingly the woody nightshade, *S. dulcamara*. It was this close relationship to some very poisonous plants that made many northern Europeans view the so-called love apple with great suspicion when it was first introduced. Indeed it

38

was described by Carl Linnaeus as *Solanum lycopersicum*, *lycopersicum* being a reference to the dangerous sounding wolf-peach. The tomato was later given its own genus by Philip Miller, who called it *Lycopersicon esculentum*. Today however botanists have classified tomatoes back within the genus *Solanum*. They are in fact so closely related to potatoes that a tomato plant can flourish when grafted onto a potato.

The tomato was first described in Europe in 1544 by the Italian Pietro Andrea Matthioli in his herbal encyclopaedia Discorsi as *mala aurea* or golden apple. A second edition of the book ten years later also referred to a red variety and it seems likely that several different forms of the fruit, some small and others large and lumpy, were introduced. In the Mediterranean countries of Spain and Italy it was quickly taken up as a welcome addition to the diet. New varieties arose by natural cross-pollination and those with particular virtues were selected to suit specific needs. The popular rotund red fruits that fill so many supermarket shelves are just one product of what is an extremely diverse plant with even conservative estimates suggesting that there are more than 5,000 cultivated varieties (cultivars) grown worldwide.

The total world production has been put at over 100 million tons a year, with tomatoes representing one of the most important of horticultural crops. Most commercial production relies on F1 hybrids which are developed to produce reliable crops of fruit of regular shape and size suitable for mechanical harvesting and ease of transport. Resistance to pests and diseases is also of prime importance. For amateur growers the benefits of F1 hybrids are also obviously of importance, but there is also a great interest in growing heirloom cultivars.

There is no set definition as to what constitutes an heirloom tomato although the term implies one that has been passed down from generation to generation within a community. Many so-called heirloom cultivars are actually quite recent creations but have attracted the 'heirloom' title as they are unlikely to be commercially successful, and so their survival depends on interested gardeners saving their seed. There has been a great resurgence of interest in heirloom varieties over the last few years with their particular qualities being celebrated at tomato festivals such as those at Carmel in the USA, West Dean in England and at Château de la Bourdaisière in France. The most famous of tomato festivals though

Grow It Yourself

is the world's biggest food fight, the festival at Buñol near Valencia in Spain that takes place on the last Wednesday of each August. The tomato fight is part of a week long fiesta of parties, concerts, fireworks and cookery demonstrations involving some 20,000 participants and several truckloads of tomatoes.

Tomatoes are short-lived perennial plants in the tropics but are grown as annuals in temperate regions. They range in size from tiny plants such as 'Micro Tom' that may be just 15cm (6in) tall to vines that can reach 10m (30ft) in a season, although 2.5m (8ft) would be more usual. There are three main types of growth habit; cordon, bush and dwarf.

Cordon tomatoes, also know as vine or indeterminate varieties, have one main vigorous stem that will continue to flower and produce fruit over a long season until it is killed by frost. The long fruiting season of cordon plants makes them particularly popular with the home gardener, but they do need sideshoots to be regularly removed. There is a greater range of fruit shapes and colours available in cordon forms.

Bush tomatoes, also called determinates as they usually grow to a fixed height, have no prominent leading shoot. A number of side branches will grow out giving a bushy plant which may sprawl on the ground. Bush types stop growing earlier than cordons with the stems ending in a fruit truss. Many paste and canning varieties are of this type as all the fruit is produced together making harvesting easier, although for small-scale domestic use this may result in a glut. Bush tomatoes are often popular for growing outdoors as the smaller plant size means it is easier to cover them with fleece in inclement weather.

Dwarf tomatoes such as 'Tiny Tim' and 'Tumbler' have a dwarfing gene which results in compact plants that are ideally suited to growing in pots or hanging baskets. Cultivars like 'Micro-Tom' are even small enough to be grown on the kitchen windowsill so that you can grow tomatoes without having a garden at all. Most of the dwarf varieties produce equally dainty tomatoes and when full of fruit they can be very ornamental.

A small number of tomato cultivars such as 'Glacier' and 'Tondino di Manduria' cannot make up their mind how they want to grow. These forms, known as semi-bush or semi-determinates, have a growth habit that is intermediate between that of a bush and a cordon type. They have vigorous lateral shoots that usually terminate in a flowering truss. They can be grown as cordons, although naturally they would usually reach a set height like the bush tomatoes, but may then produce a second crop of fruit.

Knowing when to sow your tomato seeds is not a precise science but generally aim to start them 6-8 weeks before the usual final frost date for your area. Sowing too early may result in lanky seedlings if there is insufficient light available for them. If you only want a few plants, sow just a couple of seeds in a 7-9cm (3-4in) pot. For larger quantities you can sow seed in modules or seed trays, pricking seedlings out into individual pots once they have their first true leaves. Seed germination usually takes from around 5 days at 22°C (70°F) but some older cultivars and any seed that has been stored for a long time may take 2-3 weeks.

Tomatoes are usually planted out when flowers on the lower truss are visible and once all danger of frost is over. Plants started off in a protected environment will need hardening off first. Tomatoes are gross feeders so prepare the ground well, incorporating plenty of organic matter. Water regularly to avoid problems such as fruit splitting and blossom end rot. Plants in containers will need frequent watering and supplementary feeding with a tomato fertiliser.

Make sure that you have a suitable support system ready that is appropriate for the growth habit of your chosen cultivars. In a glasshouse bamboo canes or strings tied to the roof struts may be sufficient but outdoors and for heavy cropping cultivars a sturdy stake may be required.

Many growers use wire cages made from circles of pig netting or concrete-reinforcing wire. They are particularly useful for bushy plants and can be re-used many times. Tomatoes are naturally trailing vines that will produce many sideshoots that sprawl over surrounding vegetation. In cultivation all these side shoots are removed from indeterminate plants to produce a single cordon that is easier to manage with better access of air and water to the fruit. Side shoots are formed at every leaf axil and should be regularly pinched out as soon as they are large enough to be handled. In very hot summers when there is a danger of the fruits being scorched by the sun, the side shoots can be allowed to produce one leaf each, providing additional foliage to protect the tomatoes from sun damage.

Side shoots can be a useful source of new plants if you decide that you do not have enough or want to give a favourite variety to a friend. As soon as a side shoot is reasonably firm at the base it can be snapped off and put in a glass of water to root. Research in The Netherlands has suggested that rooting is fastest when brown glass is used, so little medicine bottles are ideal containers, but side shoots will generally start to root within a week anyway. Once the roots are a few centimetres long the cuttings can be potted up and treated as any young plants.

In order for a tomato fruit to form, the stigma or female part of a flower must receive viable pollen. Cultivated forms of

the tomato are self-fertile, that is they can set fruit with their own pollen. Generally no outside intervention is required for pollination. When the flower opens pollen simply falls from the anther cone onto the stigma. However, if the atmosphere is too dry the pollen will not stick to the stigma and in very wet conditions the pollen clumps to the anthers and is not released. The optimal temperature for pollination is 18-27°C (65-80°F). At temperatures less than 10°C (50°F) very little fruit will set, whilst very high temperatures of around 40°C (105°F) will kill the pollen. It used to be common to spray plants with water to improve set in dry conditions but this can increase the incidence of fungal diseases. Many commercial units use small colonies of bumblebees (*Bombus terrestris*) in cardboard hives to fly around and distribute the pollen. You can assist with pollination yourself by gently shaking the flower clusters. The best time to do this is around noon when the pollen is most abundant.

Tomatoes are prone to a number of pests, diseases and disorders. Outdoors the most serious problem is likely to be late blight, which is caused by the fungus-like pathogen *Phytophthora infestans* and was the disease responsible for the Irish potato famine in the mid-nineteenth century. It can have a similar devastating effect on tomato crops, particu-

Tip!

In very hot summers when there is a danger of the fruits being scorched by the sun, the side shoots can be allowed to produce one leaf each, providing additional foliage to protect the tomatoes from sun damage.

larly in cool, wet climates. Spores are released from infected plants and can travel several miles in the air to initiate infection in other plants. Infected tomato plants will first show lesions on leaves, stem or fruit, but spread is rapid and complete defoliation can occur within a matter of days. The pathogen requires a living host so remove and burn any affected plants at the first sign of infection and clear away any plant debris. Do not leave potatoes in the soil at the end of the season as they can be a source of infection to subsequent crops. If you do not raise your own tomatoes from seed, check carefully to ensure you only buy in healthy stock. Growing tomatoes in a greenhouse or polytunnel will provide some protection from wind blown spores. There are few blight-tolerant tomato cultivars, although cherry tomatoes such as 'Sungold' tend to be more resistant. 'Fantasio', 'Ferline', 'Legend', and the plum tomatoes 'King Humbert' and 'San Marzano' are worth trying.

Most modern F1 hybrid tomato cultivars are relatively disease-resistant as commercial plant breeders work to improve resistance to a number of fungal and other pathogens. *Verticillium* (V) and *fusarium* (F) wilts for example are soil-borne diseases that cause yellowing of the leaves, wilting and premature death of plants. These diseases will persist in the soil where susceptible plants are grown and once they build up, the only practical control is the use of resistant varieties. Such varieties, for example 'Roma' and 'Supersweet 100', are often designated by the letters "VF" in seed catalogues. "VFN" indicates that the variety (eg. 'Lemon Boy' and 'Beefmaster') is also resistant to root-knot nematodes, worm-like pests that live in the soil.

Pests include whitefly, thrips and red spider mite, all of which are more likely to be a problem in tomatoes grown under cover. In the USA and Canada the tomato hornworm (the caterpillar of the five-spotted hawkmoth, *Manduca quinquemaculata*) can totally defoliate plants in a very short

Tip!

If you want to save seed from open-pollinated varieties, use ripe or even overripe fruits.

time. Chewed leaves in my own garden are usually a sign that the geese have wanted some variety in their diet.

If you want to save seed from open-pollinated varieties, use ripe or even overripe fruits. If you want just a few seeds they can be simply left to dry on a plate, but spread them out well so they do not go mouldy. For larger quantities growers generally use the fermentation method which removes the gel that surrounds tomato seeds and reduces the number of seed-borne diseases such as bacterial spot and early blight. Scoop seeds and gel into a jar and leave in a warm place. After a couple of days they will start to smell yeasty which indicates that fermentation is taking place. After around 5 days a white fungal layer will have formed on the surface. Scoop this off and check if gel is still present around the seeds, which would indicate the fermentation process is not complete. If the seeds have turned dark brown it has gone on too long, but the seed should still be viable. Rinse the seed well, either in the jar or through an old sieve. Spread them on a plate or tray and leave to dry for about a week before packing in paper envelopes.

Tomato Cultivars

Ailsa Craig (cordon - 68 days)

A reliable favourite for standard red, very uniform tomatoes which weigh around 90g (3½ oz) each. It is named after the isle in the Firth of Clyde.

Amana Orange (cordon - 80 days)

A large fruited cultivar with rich orange, beautifully ribbed tomatoes that average around 600g (1½ lb).

Grow It Yourself

Black Cherry (cordon - high yielding but prone to splitting, 65 days)

A popular cultivar producing big clusters of dusky deep purplish cherry tomatoes around 20-25g (¾-1oz). They are richly flavoured.

Broad Ripple Yellow Currant (cordon - 75 days)

A prolific producer of small, sweet, yellow cherry tomatoes that weigh just 8-10g (⅓oz)each and are perfect for children to nibble straight off the vine like sweets.

Cherokee Purple (cordon - 80 days)

The richly flavoured dusky maroon fruits may stay green at the shoulders. They vary from 150-400g (6-16oz). Plants show some tolerance to blight.

Coeur de Boeuf (cordon - 80 days)

A French cultivar whose name translates as ox heart, a reference to the shape of the fruits. The well flavoured meaty tomatoes average around 400g (16oz) and have few seeds.

Colgar (cordon - 85 days)

Named from the Spanish word colgar, meaning to hang, this very thick skinned pinkish-orange tomato is hung in bunches in a cool dry place in its native Catalonia and the Balearic Islands and will stay fresh and edible throughout the winter and sometimes for up to a year.

Costoluto Genovese (cordon - 78 days)

Costoluto means ribbed in Italian, a reference to the shape of these big, beautifully ruffled tomatoes that weigh around 250g (10oz). They were one of the first kinds of tomatoes to be introduced into Europe. 'Costoluto Fiorentino' is closely related but usually not so fluted in shape. Traditionally used in Italy for tomato purees, they are also ideal for pizzas and juicing.

Cream Sausage (bush - 73 days)

Commercialised by Kees Sahin of The Netherlands as 'Cream Sausage'. The novelty fruits are light yellow and long with a nipple-shaped edge. They have a mild flavour.

Delicious (cordon - 78 days)

This cultivar holds the Guinness World Record for the heaviest tomato for a fruit grown by Gordon Graham of Oklahoma that weighed in at 3.51kg (7lb 12oz), although you are more likely to get fruits weighing around 800g (1lb 12oz). Very big fruits tend not to be as flavourful as the cultivar name would suggest.

Earl of Edgecombe (cordon - 73 days)

The deep orange round tomatoes have a good flavour and few seeds.

Elberta Girl (bush - 80 days)

The foliage is densely covered with fine silver hairs and the stripy red and gold fruits have a peach-like furriness. It has to be said that the taste can be somewhat disappointing. Seed is sometimes sold as 'Elberta Peach'.

'Cream Sausage' (top)
'Elberta Girl' (middle)
'Cherokee Purple' (bottom)

Grow It Yourself

Essex Wonder (cordon - 75 days)

A vigorous English cultivar for unheated glasshouses or outdoors. Some strains of a variable nature are around. It is a potato leaf variety with firm textured scarlet fruit of a good flavour. It can be rampant when planted in the ground but is good for tubs or grow bags.

Gardener's Delight AGM (cordon - 75 days)

One of the best known of all tomatoes (sometimes under the name 'Sugar Lump') for the greenhouse or outdoors. Large cherry tomatoes are reliably produced in trusses of up to 20 fruits and have an excellent old-fashioned flavour.

Green Bell Pepper (cordon - 75 days)

This cultivar has unusual green and yellow striped hollow tomatoes with a firm flesh very like that of a bell pepper. They are ideal for stuffing with a savoury filling or used sliced into rings for salads.

Green Zebra (cordon - 75 days)

The smooth round fruits of this cultivar are orange-yellow with deep green stripes. They have a very pleasant tangy flavour.

Matt's Wild Cherry (cordon - 70 days)

An early cropping currant-type tomato of Mexican origin. It is a vigorous sprawling plant producing masses of tiny rich red tomatoes that weigh less than 3g each. They have a firm texture, an intense sweetness and contain lots of seeds. Plants will often self-seed in the garden.

Micro-Tom (dwarf - 65 days)

'Micro-Tom' forms tiny plants with equally miniature fruit, ideal for planting in a pot on the kitchen windowsill. The yellow-fruited 'Micro-Gold', 'Micro-Tina' (red) and 'Micro-Gemma' (yellow) are more recent releases with sweeter fruit. All are open-pollinated cultivars.

Omar's Lebanese (cordon - 80 days)

Vigorous plants produce very tasty pinkish-red beefsteak tomatoes that can be over 1kg (2lb) in weight, with some fruits double that.

Principe Borghese (bush - 75 days)

A good long-keeping variety with heavy clusters of small plum shaped fruit around 50g (2oz) each. The plant needs staking due to the sheer weight of fruit produced.

Reisetomate (cordon - 65 days)

Bizarre lobed fruits which look like bunches of cherry tomatoes stuck together in the manner of Siamese twins. Traditionally said to have been eaten by travellers breaking off one piece at a time.

Silvery Fir Tree (bush - 58 days)

Distinctive, finely dissected foliage, making an ornamental patio plant. The very juicy round red tomatoes have a tart flavour and lots of seeds.

Speckled Roman (cordon - 85 days)

Produces beautiful pointed plum tomatoes with stripes and speckles and a firm, meaty flesh.

Sun Baby (cordon - prolific with trusses of 50 fruits - 68 days)

Sweet, golden yellow cherry tomatoes. They are prone to splitting but are very juicy with an excellent flavour. Plants are best grown in a greenhouse but will produce a good crop against a sunny wall.

Tigerella AGM (cordon - 60 days)

An English red and yellow striped cultivar breed sometimes called 'Mr Stripey' which is actually the name of an American striped beefsteak. It usually does better under cover except in very warm summers.

'Principe Borghese' (top)
'Sunbaby' (bottom)

Tondino di Manduria
(semi-bush - 70 days)

Plants produce huge trusses of small plum tomatoes with a nipple-shaped end. Fruits often take on a pretty heart shape. They are juicier and more richly flavoured than many other plum-type tomatoes, including the widely grown 'Roma'.

Tumbling Tom Red
(bush - ideal for containers - 78 days)

The plants have a cascading growth habit. There is also a yellow version with equally small, sweet cherry tomatoes.

White Wonder (cordon - ivory coloured fruits that weigh 400-600g - 85 days)

Produce a good crop of large fruits that have a firm flesh and a mild, sweet flavour.

Yellow Stuffer (cordon - 85 days)

This cultivar closely resembles a yellow bell pepper. It is regarded as lacking in taste but ideal for stuffing.

Zapotec (cordon - fruits weigh around 300g - 80 days)

This heavily ruffled cultivar is more tolerant of drought than most tomatoes. The fruits have a very good flavour.

Storing Your Harvest

Faced with a glut of tomatoes, the easiest way to deal with them is to open freeze them then transfer to freezer bags. On thawing, tomatoes will dissolve into a mush but they will be fine for using in soups, sauces and other cooked dishes. Freezing them also makes skinning much easier; on taking them out, drop them into cold water for a few moments and the skins can then be easily peeled off. With raw tomatoes the easiest way to skin them is to cut a cross in the blossom end and plunge them into boiling water until the skin starts to curl back. Hold them under the cold tap and the skin should then peel off easily.

'Tondino di Maduria' (top)
'Silvery Fir Tree' (bottom)

Sun-dried tomatoes have been prepared in Italy for centuries as a method of storing tomatoes for the winter. Plum tomatoes are usually used as they have a drier flesh and few seeds, but any tomato cultivar is worth experimenting with. Choose tomatoes of a uniform size so they dry at the same rate. Cherry tomatoes are dried whole. Sprinkle lightly with salt and cover with a fine muslin to keep insects off.

In less favoured climates tomatoes can easily be dried in the oven. Halve the fruits and spread them out on a baking sheet. Put in the oven on its lowest setting, wedge the door ajar and leave for eight hours. Dried tomatoes can be packed into sterilised jars with bay leaves and garlic, covered with olive oil and stored for up to a year.

Tomato sauces and ketchups are extremely popular and the home-made versions are usually much tastier than commercial products. Ketchups are generally made from plum or the standard globe tomatoes. Make sure the fruits are well ripened to give the deepest colour. Onions, sweet peppers and garlic are the other main ingredients.

At the end of the season those tomatoes which have not ripened are often used in chutneys, usually made with equal quantities of cooking apples, with onions, mustard seeds and spices for flavour. Tomatoes can, however, be used in sweet preserves such as green tomato mincemeat or with ginger in jams and combined with apples or lemons in marmalades.

Cucumbers

The well known saying 'as cool as a cucumber' perfectly sums up this popular salad crop. Cucumbers are one of the crispest, most refreshing of vegetables and are much used in cosmetics to cool and sooth the skin and as slices to refresh the eyes. Although usually considered to be a vegetable, cucumbers are botanically fruits as they develop from a flower and have an enclosed seed. They are members of the plant family *Cucurbitaceae* which also includes melons, pumpkins and gourds, commonly called cucurbits. Most family members are annual vines that climb by means of tendrils.

The species *Cucumis sativus* is believed to be native to the Himalayan region of India and is thought to have been cultivated for at least three thousand years. The Roman Emperor Tiberius was said to have been particularly fond of cucumbers and ate them all year round. Fruits were grown for him in wheeled frames that could be moved into the sunshine and in special houses glazed with thin sheets of mica for the winter months. They were supposedly first introduced to England in the early 14th century.

In Tudor times some authorities thought that eating raw food caused diseases and cucumbers developed a reputation for being fit only for cows. For many years they were therefore sometimes known

Grow It Yourself

Tip!

Surplus seed can be kept for another year as stored seed usually lasts for six years or more.

as cowcumbers. The diary entry of Samuel Pepys for 22nd August 1663 records that he was told that Mr Newburne 'is dead of eating cowcumbers'. They must, however, have still been regularly grown because in Swift's Gulliver's Travels of 1726, a man in the Grand Academy of Lagado had worked for eight years on a project to extract sunbeams from cucumbers "which were to be put into Vials hermetically sealed, and let out to warm the air in raw inclement Summers"; a wonderful story of an early search for a source of alternative energy. Cucumbers were very popular in Victorian times and most big estates would have had a cucumber house devoted to their cultivation. Very few still survive, although one can be seen at the National Trust property Calke Abbey in Derbyshire.

Today cucumbers are popular right across the globe. They were taken to Russia in the 13th century and form an important part of the diet. Salted cucumber is a popular appetizer there. The International Cucumber Festival is held in Suzhal to the northeast of Moscow. In America they have been particularly popular as pickles, although in recent years consumption of pickles has declined whilst that of fresh cucumbers has increased. In China and Japan they are commonly cooked in soups as well as eaten raw and yellow cucumbers are often used to make pickles there. China produces around 60% of the world's commercial cucumbers and gherkins. A recent development is the orange-fleshed cucumber that has resulted from crosses between American pickling cucumber varieties and the orange-fruited 'Xishuangbanna' cucumber traditionally culti-vated by the Hani people of China.

Commercial production usually relies on all-female F1 hybrids which are suited to intensive production, giving earlier cropping and greater disease resistance, so there is less need for the use of fungicides. Whilst in some countries cucumbers are grown as a field crop, in the United Kingdom protected cropping is usual. Seedlings are generally grown by specialist plant raisers in early winter and are transferred to the produc-tion greenhouse in December or January. They are mostly grown in rockwool, which is a sterile substance reducing the likelihood of disease. Plants are kept at a minimum of 21°C (70°F) and are ventilated if temperatures reach 24°C (75°F). They are usually trained as cordons up strings to a horizontal support wire about 2m (6ft) above the ground. Side shoots are removed until the leader shoot reaches this wire, then the leader is pinched out and three strong laterals chosen to cascade down.

For the home gardener cucumbers may be grown as protected crops in greenhouses, polytunnels or cold frames. There are however also a large number of cultivars that can be grown successfully outdoors in the vegetable garden or even in pots or grow bags on the patio. Cucumbers have a reputation for being difficult to grow and many old textbooks are full of complicated instructions about humidity requirements, training on horizontal wires, identifying male and female flowers and alarming lists of pests and diseases. However, with the advent of modern F1 cultivars, especially the all-female flowered forms, growing cucumbers has become much simpler.

Sow seed in early spring in 9cm (3½in) pots of standard seed compost. It is usual to recommend sowing two seeds per pot and then removing the weakest seedling, but given the high price of F1 hybrid seed I generally sow seeds individually. They normally germinate in just 6-10 days so you do not lose too much time if you have to re-sow to make up for any that fail to germinate. Any surplus seed can be kept for another year as stored seed usually lasts for six years or more.

Keep pots of seed at around 20-26°C (68-79°F) until they germinate. An

airing cupboard or sunny windowsill usually works well. Seedlings can be grown on at slightly lower temperatures of around 18-21°C (64-70°F). Transplant seedlings intended for protected cultivation into 25cm (10in) pots, grow bags or well manured beds once they have their first true leaves and so long as you can maintain temperatures of around 15-20°C (60-70°F). Space plants around 60cm (24in) apart in beds. If you are using grow bags allow just one or two plants per bag to maximise the crop produced. Plants in pots are best grown in a John Innes type compost. Support the plants with bamboo canes or strings. Train the main shoot vertically up the support and pinch out the tip when it reaches about 1.5m (55in). All-female cultivars bear fruits on the main stem so remove any side shoots. Older cultivars will need horizontal wire supports.

Outdoor cucumbers were also widely known as ridge cucumbers as they were usually grown on the mounds of ridged beds, which warm up quicker and have better drainage. They can also be grown successfully in a normal flat bed. Seedlings will need to be hardened off and can be transplanted outside in early summer when all danger of frost has passed. Space them around 60cm (24in) apart in soil to which lots of organic matter has been added to help retain moisture. Pinch out the tip once they have six or seven leaves to encourage the formation of sideshoots and production of lots of fruits. Plants can be allowed to trail or may be trained up supports. If they are to be trained up a trellis or netting, space the plants 45cm (18in) apart and stop them at the top of the support.

After planting out regular watering is essential to help plants establish. Keep the growing material moist but do not allow it to become water-logged, as that would encourage basal rots. Feed plants every two weeks once the first fruits start to swell. Feed with a high potash, tomato type fertilizer or an equivalent organic liquid feed. In cold conditions it may be worth mulching outdoor plants with black polythene which helps to warm the soil as well as keeping the weeds down. The herb tansy (*Tanacetum vulgare*) is sometimes recommended as a companion plant for cucumbers as it is thought to repel the cucumber beetle which is a serious pest in parts of the United States.

The older outdoor cucumbers are monoecious which means that they bear separate male and female flowers on the same plant. The female flowers can be readily identified as they carry miniature cucumbers just behind the flower. If few insects are around you may need to hand pollinate these flowers; use a small paint brush to transfer pollen from the male flowers to the female ones. At the start of the season some cucumbers may only produce male flowers. The female flowers and fruit should follow as the weather warms up.

Greenhouse cucumbers are generally parthenocarpic; that is, in contrast to outdoor types, the female flowers do not need to be pollinated in order to produce fruit. Indeed, if they are pollinated the resulting cucumbers may taste bitter. Older varieties will have male flowers and these should be removed to prevent pollination. All-female F1 hybrids do not ordi-narily produce male flowers, although if plants are stressed by inappro-priate growing conditions some male flowers may then be produced. Do not grow the ridge type cucumbers in a greenhouse alongside all-female cultivars or cross-pollination will occur.

Harvest cucumbers by cutting the fruit with secateurs or a sharp knife once the fruit reaches a reasonable size. Gherkins are harvested when they are 2.5-7cm long (1-3in) or once they have reached a suitable size for pickling. If you leave fruits on the vine for too long the production of more fruits will cease.

Given the high price of F1 hybrid cucumber seed it is worth raising extra cucumber plants from cuttings which enables them to be kept on from year to year. Take a shoot which is ready for stopping, cutting it off below a leaf joint, remove the lower leaf from the shoot and insert the cutting into a pot of compost about 2cm (1in) deep. Keep the cutting warm and moist and shade it from hot sun until it is well rooted. It is useful to cover the cutting with a polythene bag or cut down lemonade bottle to retain humidity. Cuttings taken early in the season can produce fruits by the autumn. Autumn cuttings can be overwintered in a frost-free greenhouse or on a cool windowsill to give plants for next season.

Many modern cucumbers are seedless and so saving seed from them is not an option. However, for older and open-pollinated cultivars it is well worth saving seed yourself. Cucumbers do cross-pollinate readily so if you grow more than one variety it is important to protect the flower of your chosen variety with a piece of old stocking or muslin bag to prevent accidental pollination by insects. You will then have to hand pollinate that flower. When intended for seed collection the cucumbers need to be ripened well beyond the edible stage, so towards the end of the growing season leave one or two on the vine. They will become much fatter and green varieties will turn a deep yellowish-brown colour, whilst white varieties generally turn yellow. Keep them for a week or so after picking to let the seeds mature fully. Cut the fruit open and scoop the seeds and surrounding pulp into a glass jar, adding a little water. Leave the jar on a sunny windowsill for 2-3 days for the seeds to ferment. This helps to kill any harmful bacteria. Then top the jar up with water and stir well. The good seeds should sink to the bottom of the jar, leaving the pulp and debris floating on top. Gently pour off the water and debris and rinse the seeds in clean water. Spread the seeds out on a plate or old chopping board to dry.

When it comes to choosing which cultivars to grow, the selection of plants at many garden centres is often extremely limited. However, so long as you are prepared to grow plants yourself from seed the choice will be greater. Most of the major seed companies list a selection of glasshouse and outdoor varieties including some standard long green cucumbers, a couple of mini salad types, one or two pickling cultivars and if you are

lucky a selection of the more unusual coloured cultivars. Which you choose depends on the facilities you have available, what you intend to use the fruits for and, of course, personal preference.

If you just want plenty of cucumbers for family salads, choose any of the all-female hybrids if you have a greenhouse or polytunnel. For the open garden a ridge type such as 'Marketmore' or 'Burpless Tasty Green' is best. For bitter-free fruits try the newer introductions such as 'Bella' or 'Prima Top'. Bitterness in cucumbers results from the presence of the intensely bitter compounds cucurbitacins, which are thought to have evolved to protect the plants from herbivores. Cucumbers are more likely to be bitter if plants are stressed, particularly in high temperatures or when there is insufficient water available. For exhibition purposes 'Carmen', 'Femdan' and 'Bodega' are reliable producers of quality fruit. Of course if you are planning to break records you will need to search out specialist seed of cultivars such as 'BL9 Mammoth'. The Guinness World Record for the longest cucumber was set by Alf Cobb of Nottinghamshire in 2008 for a fruit that measured in at 91.694cm (36in). Growing such monster vegetables requires a considerable amount of dedication. 92 year old Mr Cobb gets up daily at 5am to water his plants.

Grow It Yourself

Indoor Cucumbers

Birgit (30 fruits per plant, 32cm long)

F1 Hybrid AGM – A well known cultivar, widely grown by market gardeners and popular for exhibition.

Carmen (20 fruits per plant, 35cm long)

F1 Hybrid AGM – All-female flowered plants with good disease resistance. They crop in 60 days from sowing.

Cucino (produces lots of small fruits)

F1 Hybrid – An interesting all-female cultivar with fruits just 5-7cm (2-3in) which are very popular with children.

Ilas (heavy cropping mini-fruit)

F1 Hybrid – Very easy to grow as the side shoots stop growing at a flower cluster so do not need pinching back. It shows good resistance to powdery mildew.

Melonie

An unusual cucumber with long fruits that are striped green and white and have a distinctively flavoured sweet flesh, somewhat like a melon.

Prima Top (high yield of short fruits 20 - 22cm long)

F1 Hybrid AGM – Easy to grow, disease resistant cultivar that stays fairly compact.

Socrates (prolific crop of mini-fruits)

F1 Hybrid – An improved version of the popular cultivar 'Petita' with all-female flowers. Strong, vigorous plants, the cucumbers have smooth skins and a bitter-free flesh.

Sunsweet (prolific crop of small fruits)

F1 Hybrid – A prolific producer of small fruits the size and colour of a lemon. Pick early to eat raw or cook like a courgette once mature.

Telegraph Improved

The original cultivar 'Telegraph' dates back to at least 1848 when it was listed by Messrs Fisher, Holmes and Co, at a time when the telegraph was considered the very latest in modern technology. Improved forms have been around since 1869 or earlier and are still among the favourites for growing in cold frames. ('Telepathy' is a modern F1 version which crops earlier.)

Tiffany (fruits 28 - 35cm long)

F1 Hybrid – All-female flowering vigorous plants produce a good crop of slightly ribbed, deep green fruits produced over a long season. They show good resistance to powdery mildew.

Vista (heavy fruits that can reach 40cm long)

F1 Hybrid – An all-female cucumber, Vista goes on producing top quality, long, straight fruits right through to autumn. The heavy fruits are well flavoured.

Zeina (Average 60 fruits per plant)

F1 Hybrid AGM – Very productive cultivar which can average more than 60 fruits per plant. The fruits are around 20cm (8in) in length and have bright, glossy skins.

Grow It Yourself

Outdoor Cucumbers

Bimbostar (gherkin with good disease resistance)

F1 Hybrid – An all-female flower which gives an early, prolific crop of seedless fruits with tender skins, ideal for pickling or delicious raw.

Boothby's Blonde

Grown by the Boothby family for many generations and still maintained by them. It has creamy coloured fruits with tiny black spines.

Burpless Tasty Green (growing to 23cm long with resistance to mildew)

F1 Hybrid – They have a crisp and tasty flesh that is easy to digest and free from bitterness.

Crystal Apple (productive and disease resistant but bitter when mature)

An easy to grow cultivar with round yellowish fruits streaked with cream. Pick the fruits when they are just 5-7.5cm (2-3in) long when they are sweet and flavoursome.

Diamant (reliable gherkin variety producing a good early crop)

F1 Hybrid – Short firm fruits ideal for pickling. It has good resistance to both downy and powdery mildew.

Kaiser Alexander (melon shaped fruit 15cm long, stores well after havesting)

An heirloom variety with big fat fruits that look like cantaloupe melons. The skin matures to brown with a netted appearance. Very crunchy flesh with a mild sweet taste. From seed to first picking is around 60 days.

Marketmore (reliable and prolific with fruits 20cm long and mildew resistant)

AGM – Very reliable, crops around 70 days. 'Marketmore 97' is an all-female strain.

Masterpiece (early, reliable British cucumber producing straight cucumbers)

AGM – Open-pollinated, it produces plentiful crops of deep green skinned fruits that have just a few spines and crisp white flesh.

Parisian Pickling (reliable and productive, ideal for pickling)

An heirloom cultivar specially selected in Paris when cucumbers became a fashionable vegetable in the 1800s. It can be allowed to grow to a large size but would then need to be peeled.

Prima Top (vigorous plants with mostly female flowers)

F1 Hybrid AGM – The dark green, rather chubby fruits have quite smooth skins with some small white spines. They grow to around 20-22cm (8-9in) long.

Tokyo Slicer (production with fruits 30cm long)

F1 Hybrid AGM – Very productive Japanese cultivar with fruits that average 30cm (12in) long with smooth skins.

Grow It Yourself

Venlo Pickling (gherkin)

Raised at the Venlo research station in the southeastern Netherlands, this cultivar produces masses of small tender fruit throughout the summer.

White Wonder (small vines, making it ideal for patios)

A very old cucumber also known as 'Long White' and thought to be the same as the Italian plant known as 'Mezzo Lungo Bianco'. It was introduced to America through the seed company Burpees in 1893. Traditionally used for pickling, it can also be harvested as a slicing variety to pick at about 15cm (6in) long.

Novelties

Carosello Mezzo Lungo di Polignano

In the Puglia region of southeast Italy the immature fruits of many melons (Cucumis melo) are eaten as bitter-free alternatives to cucumber. The group known as carosello (which translates as carousel) includes this variety from Polignano, a fortified city overlooking the Adriatic. The oval fruits are 10 to 15cm long (4-6in) with a corrugated skin covered in woolly fuzz. The flesh is crisp with a distinct melon flavour. It matures in 50-60 days.

Exploding Hedgehogs (vigorous climbing vine)

Plant outdoors after all danger of frost has passed or under cover. The small fruits resemble miniature boxing gloves and are covered in spines, like baby hedgehogs. Eat raw when just a centimetre long. When the fruits mature they will burst open at the slightest touch, flinging their seed halfway across the garden. The Spanish name of 'Ojo ciego', which means blind eye, should be treated as a serious warning!

Gemsbok Cucumber (spherical fruits maturing from green to orange)

A perennial plant with thick, fleshy roots from which grow annual stems up to 6m long which normally trail along the ground and often form roots at the nodes. The stems carry spiny tendrils and lobed leaves. They are covered with prominent spines. The fruits are perfectly edible but do not have the most appetising of tastes.

Peruvian Wild Cucumber (up to 20cm long fruits, hollow inside)

One of the so-called 'lost crops of the Incas', this attractive vine has whorls of bright green leaves and long tendrils. They are widely grown in Asia where they are eaten both raw and cooked as immature fruits. The young shoots and leaves can also be eaten as a green vegetable.

Storing Your Harvest

For pickled cucumbers wash 2kg (4lb) of cucumbers. Keep small gherkins whole but chop larger fruits into 1cm (¼in) slices. Put in a large bowl with a sliced onion, half a cup of salt and four cups of iced water and leave to stand, preferably overnight. Heat three cups of cider vinegar, one cup of sugar, two teaspoons of mustard seed and one teaspoon of turmeric in a large pan. Add the rinsed and drained vegetables and boil for five minutes before packing into hot jars with some of the syrup.

Peppers

Peppers have a very ancient association with man and are thought to be one of the oldest cultivated crops. Archaeologists in South America have identified microscopic starch grains unique to chillies which were found on cooking implements dating back 6,000 years. Peppers were encountered by Christopher Columbus while in the Caribbean on his first voyage to the Americas. He called them red pepper as their pungency reminded him of the black pepper, *Piper nigrum*, a totally unrelated plant. In 1493 they were further described by Diego Álvarez Chauca, a physician on Columbus's second expedition to the New World. He wrote about natives using them as a spice they called agi and for medicinal use. The Aztecs grew dozens of different types of peppers. According to the Franciscan monk Bernardino de Sahagún who lived in Mexico in 1529, there were "hot green chiles, smoked chiles, water chiles, tree chiles, beetle chiles, and sharp-pointed red chiles".

The botanical name for peppers, *Capsicum*, comes from the Latin word *capsa* meaning a box, which is a reference to the hollow, box-like shape of the sweet pepper. Opinions vary widely on the taxonomy of the genus *Capsicum*, but there are generally accepted to be between 20 and 30 wild species and five so-called domesticated species which have given rise to the different forms of peppers in cultivation.

It is the two species *C. annuum* and *C. frutescens*

that have produced the majority of cultivated peppers which are grown for their fruits. The fruits are botanically large berries. Cultivars of *C. annuum* include the sweet peppers, *C. annuum Grossum* Group, and the chilli peppers, *C. annuum Longum* Group. Both types are annual plants growing to around 75cm (30in). Sweet peppers come in a variety of shapes and are often known as bell or bullnose peppers because of their resemblance to those shapes. They start green, ripening to red, yellow, creamy white, orange, purple or brown depending on the cultivar. Chilli peppers usually have narrow, pointed fruits which ripen to red and a hot taste that intensifies as the fruit matures. Hot peppers are mostly cultivars of the species *C. frutescens* and include those known as cayenne, Tabasco peppers and the spur pepper, so-called because it resembles a cockerel's spur. They are perennial plants but are usually grown as annuals. They can reach 1.5m (5ft) tall and produce small, highly pungent fruits. They need a long growing season and so tend to do better in the south.

Other domesticated species include the so-called tree pepper *C. pubescens*, which can grow to around 3m (10ft) tall. It is hardy to −5°C (23°F) and may live for 15 years or more in cool temperate climates. Known as rocoto or locoto, the fruits are fairly small and round with thick fleshy walls and a pungent taste. Cultivated varieties of *C. baccatum* are commonly called ají in South America. They have a distinctive fruity taste that is favoured for the marinated fish dish ceviche. *C. chinense* was so named because the Dutch botanist Nikolaus Joseph von Jacquin believed that they came from China, although like other capsicums they are actually of American origin, being found in the West Indies, Central America and northern South America. Selections of this species include some of the world's hottest chillis such as the variously coloured habanero cultivars and the Jamaican 'Scotch Bonnet' with lantern-shaped fruits that have a smoky flavour.

The active heat-producing component of chilli and other hot peppers is a group of chemicals called capsaicinoids, primarily capsaicin, a bitter, acrid alkaloid. The presence of capsaicin depends on a single gene and cultivars without that gene have sweet fruits. The concentration of capsaicin in chilli fruit is chiefly goverened by the genetic makeup of a particular cultivar, but levels are also influenced by growing conditions and the maturity of the fruit. Some cultivars such as the Pimientos de Padron have earned themselves the nickname of Russian roulette chillis as most of the fruits on an individual plant can be quite mild, but there is the occasional fruit which is extremely hot.

Pepper seeds themselves do not produce any capsaicin but the highest concentration is found in the white pith around the seeds. Capsaicin is thought to have evolved as an antifungal agent to protect the seeds from *Fusarium* type fungi that are spread by sap sucking bugs. Studies in Bolivia showed that where hemiptera bugs are more common the peppers growing in those areas had higher levels of capsaicin.

The presence of capsaicin in peppers is also of benefit for their seed dispersal. Pepper seeds eaten by mammals usually do not germinate whereas those consumed by birds pass through the digestive tract undamaged. Capsaicin is an irritant to mammals including man, producing a burning sensation by binding with chemoreceptor nerve endings in the skin, particularly the mucous membranes. Birds, however, lack the chemical receptors to detect capsaicin and therefore can eat hot peppers with impunity. The presence of capsaicin therefore may be a way of discouraging mammals from eating the fruits, leaving seed dispersal to the birds.

The heat of a pepper is measured in Scoville Heat Units (SHU), named in honour of the American chemist Wilbur Scoville who in 1902 developed a method for measuring the amount of capsaicin in a given pepper. Originally this involved tasting a diluted version of a pepper and giving it a value. Nowadays it can be done more accurately with the help of computers to measure the amount of capsaicin present in parts per million. A measurement of one part capsaicin per million corresponds to about 15 Scoville units. The Scoville scale begins at zero with mild bell peppers ranging to an SHU of 16,000,000 for pure capsaicin. The jalapeño pepper is a medium hot pepper with a range of about 2,500 to 5,000 Scoville units. Chillis such as cayenne and ají rate at about 30,000 to 50,000 units, while the habernero, which is one of the hottest, comes somewhere between 100,00 and 500,000 units. The heat of a chilli pepper will depend not just on the cultivar but also on how it is grown. Plants that are stressed by insufficient water or pest attack will produce more capsaicin.

Capsaicin is a potent chemical that survives both cooking and freezing.

It is not water-soluble so having a drink of water to try and reduce the heat of consumed peppers will have only a temporary cooling effect. Dairy products such as milk are more effective as the casein they contain acts as a detergent, removing the capsaicin from the nerve receptors. Milk chocolate, beans and nuts are also recommended. Apart from the burning sensation capsaicin also triggers the brain to produce endorphins, natural painkillers that promote a sense of well-being.

Peppers are members of the *Solanaceae* along with potatoes, tomatoes and aubergines and so are included with those vegetables in crop rotation schemes. They are however usually healthier than tomatoes and are less susceptible to blight. They also require less feeding and can generally be grown easily in pots and grow bags. Many plants such as *C. frutescens* 'Tabasco' are extremely ornamental in fruit and are suitable for growing in pots on the patio. Flowers vary from white to shades of purple and are very pretty, often resembling miniature pendant lampshades. Cultivars such as 'Fish' and 'Purple Tiger' have attractive variegated leaves, whilst those of 'Black Hungarian' are a rich bronze when they first emerge.

If planning to grow peppers in a greenhouse or polytunnel, sow the seed from mid-February to early April. For outdoor cultivation sow around the end of March. Some cultivars such as 'Black Hungarian' will give a decent crop even if sowing is delayed as late as June. Sow seed at 18-25°C (65-77°F) in pots of good compost in a propagator or on a sunny window-sill. Seed usually takes around ten days to germinate. Transplant into individual 9cm (3½in) pots when the first two true leaves have formed. Grow on in good light and try to maintain a minimum night temperature of at least 15°C (59°F). Transfer plants to 25cm (10in) pots of good

compost in May. Plants can also be grown in grow bags but will then need more careful watering. Allow two plants per standard sized grow bag. Alternatively, if growing in a bed, plant 45cm (18in) apart. Warm outdoor soils with polythene or cloches for two weeks before putting plants out at the end of May or in early June. Keep the young plants covered with cloches or a sheet of horticultural fleece for a further couple of weeks. Peppers generally require more warmth than tomatoes and so may be best grown in a glasshouse or sheltered sunny spot.

Pinch out the growing tips of chillies when they are about 20cm (8in) tall to encourage a bushy habit. This is sometimes done to sweet peppers but it will delay cropping. Taller cultivars and those with large fruit may need to be staked to a bamboo cane and tied in as they grow. Water regularly and feed weekly with a high potassium tomato-type fertiliser once the first fruit has set. Misting the foliage regularly with water will help to discourage red spider mite and is thought to help flower set and subsequently cropping. Harvest the fruit as required when it is green, glossy and full sized. The fruit can be kept on the plant to ripen but this will slow development of subsequent fruit and reduce the total quantity of crop. At the end of the season the whole plant can be uprooted and hung in a frost-free shed to allow any remaining fruit to ripen.

Peppers are generally very healthy plants and are not prone to many pests and diseases. Aphids are the most common problem and should be controlled as they can spread tomato mosaic virus which causes mottled leaves and a general weakening of the plant. Some F1 hybrids are resistant to diseases

including tomato mosaic virus. Inspect plants regularly and rub off any aphids. Under glass red spider mites may be a problem. Watch for discoloured leaves and light webbing, particularly on shoot tips. Excessive temperatures or lack of water can cause flowers and young fruit to drop. Remove any dead leaves and maintain good air circulation to prevent grey mould (Botrytis). In cool damp conditions *sclerotinia* fungi may cause dark lesions on the lower stems. Growing peppers in pots or grow bags will prevent infection from spores present in the soil.

Tip!

Smaller cultivars such as 'Demon Red' can be grown successfully on a sunny windowsill.

Saving your own seed from peppers is very easy as the seeds are large and easy to handle. If you grow more than one cultivar it is worth isolating the plant from which you want to save seed during flowering so that it will not cross-pollinate with other varieties. Allow the fruits to ripen thoroughly, then cut them open and scrape the seed off with a blunt knife. Spread out evenly on a plate or chopping board and leave to dry for a few days, stirring from time to time to ensure that they are thoroughly dried. Seed can also be collected from dried chillies sold commercially. Remember to wash your hands thoroughly with soap after handling hot peppers and not to touch your eyes for several hours afterwards. Store the seed in paper packets in a cool, dry place. Stored seed does not always last very well so it is best used within three years.

Grow It Yourself

Sweet Pepper Cultivars

Ace (produces 15 fleshy fruits which ripen to a rich, red colour)

AGM F1 hybrid – A productive cultivar that grows to around 90cm (3ft) with plants producing an early crop. It is disease resistant and one of the best cultivars for growing outdoors.

Atris (produces 50 or more fruits up to 22cm (9in) long per plant)

AGM – An early, very productive cultivar with tall plants that produce fleshy, horn-shaped fruits They mature to a deep red.

California Wonder (each fruit is 10cm (4in) in diameter)

Dating back to 1928, this is a popular, very reliable producer of mild, sweet peppers. They ripen to red but are used as a standard green pepper.

Charleston Belle (bell shaped pappers weighing 100g (3½in))

Compact, early cropping plants developed in South Carolina, America. They produce large, smooth bell peppers and resist nematodes.

Corno di Toro Rosso (or Red Bull's Horn, produces 25 peppers per plant)

AGM – Long horn-like shape. The fleshy fruits have a good sweet flavour but can be slow to ripen. Plants grow to about 150cm (5ft).

Feherozon (conical fruits 10cm (3½in) long ripening from cream to red)

An early cropping, productive Hungarian cultivar with sweet tasting conical fruits. Traditionally dried and ground into paprika but equally good fresh in salads.

Gourmet (long season of crops)

AGM – Compact plants produce an early and prolific crop of vivid orange blocky peppers. Well worth trying outdoors.

Gypsy (20 or more fruits per plant, the plant grows to 1m (39in) high)

AGM F1 hybrid – High yielding plants with an early crop of fruits ripening from pale green to clear scarlet. They have a good, sweet flavour.

Jumbo (giant fruits weighing 200g (7oz) and measuring up to 10 x 20cm)

F1 Hybrid – Lives up to its name with giant fruits that ripen to a rich dark red. The best crops are achieved when plants are grown in a greenhouse.

King of the North (bred for short seasons as the plants grow quickly)

The plants produce large green bell fruits which turn red when mature. Flowers may fail to set fruit in very hot conditions.

Mohawk (produces around 16 medium sized, bell-shaped fruits per plant)

F1 Hybrid AGM – Plants have a compact habit, ideal for pots, window-boxes or even hanging baskets.

Sweet Chocolate (bred for cooler climates, it ripens to chocolate brown)

An unusual sweet pepper with thick reddish flesh. It is a fairly early and productive cultivar, worth trying in areas with short seasons.

Tequila Sunrise (ornamental, carrot-shaped fruits)

Golden yellow fruits with a sharp/sweet flavour. Plants usually produce the first fruits in around 70 days from transplanting.

Topboy / Topgirl (attractive globe shaped fruits 10cm (4in) in diameter)

AGM – A mid-season cultivar that produces a large crop. The fruits have a thick flesh and are good for stuffing. They mature to a bright yellow.

Unicorn (high yield with 18cm (7in) long fruits and plants can be late to fruit)

Short-growing plants. The thick-fleshed fruits ripen to bright red.

Hungarian Wax

Chilli / Hot Pepper Cultivars

Ají Lemon Drop (slow to mature and very hot)

A cultivar of the species *Capsicum baccatum* from Peru. The very attractive clear yellow fruits have a citrusy flavour.

Black Hungarian (produces a reliable crop even in poor summers)

Ornamental plants with bronze young leaves and attractive conical fruits that change from green to glossy black and then mature to deep red. They are mildly spicy. The cultivar 'Chenzo' is similar.

Black Pearl (small, bushy plants that grow to 45cm (18in) high)

It has extremely attractive deep bronze leaves and small glossy black fruits that ripen to red. Ideal for pots on the patio, the fruits are edible but are very hot, so take care if using them.

Bhut Jolokia Fiery Furnace (scarlet fruits up to 8cm (3in) long)

Strictly for those with a sense of adventure, this pepper, one of the *Capsicum chinense* type, measures 1,000,000 units on the Scoville scale.

Caldero (compact plants, ideal for window boxes or hanging baskets)

They produce a generous supply of medium hot conical fruits that change from creamy yellow through orange to red.

Habanero Orange

Demon Red (compact plants, ideal for containers)

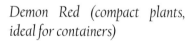

AGM – A cultivar of the species *Capsicum frutescens*. They produce many small finger-like red fruits that are very hot.

Filius Blue (fruits are hot but get milder as they mature to red)

AGM – Very ornamental small plants with purplish foliage and purple-blue fruits, ideal for growing on the patio.

Fish (first fruits are mild but as the plant matures they get very hot)

An heirloom cultivar from the African-American community of New England, USA which is very ornamental with variegated leaves. Immature fruits tend to be the most spicy and they often then mellow as the bright red colour develops.

Grow It Yourself

Friar's Hat

A cultivar of the species *Capsicum baccatum* with a tall, rambling habit. It produces intriguing shaped fruits which vary greatly in heat intensity.

Habanero Orange (One of the hottest of peppers with 3cm (1in) long fruits)

Believed to have originated in the Yucatán Peninsula of Mexico as a selection of the species *Capsicum chinense*. The chubby fruits ripen to a rich orange colour. Other coloured varieties include red, white and brown.

Navaho (medium heat intensity)

AGM – Robust plants produce many thick-fleshed red fruits. They are suitable for stuffing.

Pinocchio's Nose (heavy crop of fruits up to 25cm (10in) long - very hot!)

Also known as 'Joe's Long Cayenne' this cultivar produces slender fruits.

Sheepnose Pimiento (mild tasting fruits of 10cm (4in) that mature in 75 days)

An heirloom cultivar from Ohio in the US. They are mild tasting and quite sweet and juicy.

Summer Heat

AGM – An early fruiting jalapeño-type pepper with a hot chilli taste. The skin on the torpedo-shaped fruits tends to get corky stripes which are considered an indication of quality in Mexican cooking. It crops well even in short growing seasons.

Thai Dragon

AGM – Very vigorous plants produce prolific quantities of extremely spicy peppers that are finger shaped and bright red.

Storing Your Harvest

Be careful when handling hot peppers and take special care to ensure that you do not touch your face or eyes while working with them. Wash your hands thoroughly with soap or olive oil afterwards, as just plain water is ineffective at removing capsaicin from the skin. If using the very hot peppers it is best to wear latex gloves and to discard them afterwards. Chilli oil will cause rubber gloves to deteriorate after an hour or so.

Paprika is a spice made by grinding dried sweet red peppers. It was originally used in Hungary as a treatment for fever but became an important component of Hungarian cuisine. It gives the deep brick-red colour to goulash, the thick Hungarian stew of beef, red onions, diced potatoes and sometimes vegetables such as carrots and parsnips. A similar dish known as paprikás consists of diced meat served with a thick, rich sauce of cream and paprika. Paprika is used in Spain and Portugal for fish stews, vegetable soups and in sausages such as chorizo.

Chilli powders are dried and ground chillies and vary enormously in heat. They are much used in Creole cookery. Cayenne pepper, originally from Cayenne in French Guiana, is a very hot orange powder from ground dried chillies. It is used sprinkled over egg mayonnaise and in shellfish or game recipes. Harissa is a very hot Tunisian mixture of crushed chillies with ground cumin and salt used to add spice to couscous.

Chilli vinegar can be made by steeping whole chillies in wine vinegar for ten days, giving them a daily shake. Tabasco sauce is an exceedingly hot condiment made from vinegar, red chillies and salt. There are numerous recipes for chilli sauce, a thick hot bright red sauce used on burgers, hot dogs and with discretion as a dip for spare ribs. Most are based on tomatoes, onions, sweet red and jalapeño peppers boiled with vinegar, sugar and salt until thick.

Aubergines

The colour purple has long been associated with royalty and Louis XIV of France was so intrigued by the aubergine in its rich purple incarnation that he instructed his gardener Jean-Baptiste La Quintinie to grow it in the Potager du Roi at Versailles. Food fights were apparently all the rage at the court of King Louis, so it is debatable whether the aubergines were eaten much or purely used for ammunition. Indeed the aubergine, like the tomato, was at times viewed with suspicion in northern Europe due to its close relationship to plants such as deadly nightshade, which is also a member of the *Solanaceae* family. Many early cultivars were quite bitter in taste and eating them was said to cause insanity. The Italian name for aubergine, melanzana, comes from the Latin for 'mad apple'.

The aubergine is generally considered to be native to India, although it has been cultivated in both India and China for thousands of years, making determining its exact origin difficult. Certainly wild types with numerous small fruits are found on the Bengal plains of India. The Arabs introduced aubergines to North Africa and Spain in the Middle Ages and they were taken to the Americas by the Spanish. Aubergines were considered very exotic in Britain and Ireland before the 1950s when they started to become popular partly as a result of the writings

78

of the respected British cookery writer Elizabeth David.

The botanical name for the aubergine is *Solanum melongena*, derived from a sixteenth century Arabic word for one type of the fruit. A form with white fruits about the shape and size of a hen's egg and similar to the modern cultivars 'Ova' and 'Easter Egg', was the one most commonly grown in northern Europe in the sixteenth century and led to the use of the popular name of eggplant, which is still used instead of aubergine in the United States and Australia.

The name aubergine is of French origin and has rather a convoluted derivation. The Sanskrit name used in India vatin-ganah translates literally as 'anti-flatulence vegetable'. Vatin-ganah became badin-gan in Persian, then al-badindjan in Arabic. When the Arabs eventually introduced the fruit to Spain its name became alberginia in Catalan and finally aubergine in French. In India today and in South Africa the fruits are known as brinjal.

The aubergine is a short-lived perennial or sub-shrub that is usually grown as an annual in cooler climates. Plants have a bushy habit and generally grow to around 60-75cm (24-30in). Some cultivars have spines on the stem, leaves and calyx. It has very attractive large lobed leaves which usually have a downy texture. The leaves vary considerably between cultivars, with some plants having thick, felt-like leaves richly veined in purple, making them worth growing just as a foliage plant. The leaves of the Ethiopian eggplant, *Solanum aethiopicum*, are an important vegetable in West Africa. In Malaysia the young leaves of the so-called 'salad eggplant' are cooked in stir-fries.

Aubergines have attractive flowers that can be white or varying shades of purple with a central cone of yellow stamens. Plants are self-fertile so even a single plant grown on its own will produce fruit. Although nearly always treated as a vegetable, the aubergine is botanically classified as a fruit and is technically a berry, being a simple fruit with seeds and flesh produced from a single ovary. In Britain the most familiar aubergine is the plump, elongated pear-shaped fruit with glossy purple-black skin. However there is a wide variety of cultivars available in other shapes, sizes and colours, including many that are attractively striped. 'Japanese Pickling' 'Asian Bride' and 'Thai Long Green' have long slender fruits.

Grow It Yourself

Those of 'Bambino' and 'Ronde de Valence' are small ovals, whilst those of 'Turkish Orange', a cultivar of the species *Solanum aethiopicum*, can be perfect globes. A huge range is grown in Asia with fruits that vary from the size of a pea to mammoth specimens that can weigh up to a kilogram (2lb).

Aubergines are warm weather crops that require quite a long growing season. Growth is best at temperatures of 20-28°C (68-82°F). Plants are usually grown in a greenhouse but they may do well on a sunny patio and the smaller cultivars can even be grown as windowsill plants. They tend to require a bit more warmth than tomatoes. Plants are usually started off under cover, either in a frost-free glasshouse or on a sunny windowsill in the home. Typically seed will be sown eight to ten weeks before the anticipated last frost for your area. I have, however, had a successful crop of the cultivar 'Fairy Tale' from seed sown as late as the end of June, but sowing this late means taking a gamble on the fruit ripening before the first autumn frosts, even on plants grown under cover.

As a general guide sow seed in March at a temperature of 20-25°C (68-77°F) in an airing cupboard or propagator. Seed is usually sown in cells or individual pots of compost to minimise root disturbance on transplanting. Fresh seed will usually germinate in about a week. Older seed may take longer and can benefit from being soaked in warm water for an hour or so before sowing. Grow seedlings on at a minimum temperature of 15°C (60°F) with plenty of light for four or five weeks until they have four true leaves. Plants destined for outdoor growing should be hardened off for a week or so before planting in the garden when all danger of frost has passed.

Plant out seedlings in a green-house or polytunnel bed with a spacing of around 45cm (18in) between plants or outdoors in warmer gardens. A sandy loam is ideal although heavier soils may give a longer cropping period. Alternatively use grow bags or large pots. I use black plastic pots around 25cm (10in) in diameter (at least 7.5 litre capacity) or plastic buckets with holes drilled in for drainage. The black plastic helps to absorb heat which is beneficial to the plants. Keep pots and bags in a warm sheltered spot such as against a sunny wall. They are very attractive plants to grow cottage-style among ornamentals in a mixed border. Seedlings planted outside may need the protection of a cloche or layer of horticultural fleece until they have established and the weather has warmed up. Four pint plastic milk cartons with the bottom cut off make useful little cloches for young seedlings.

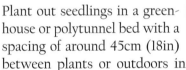

Tip!

Four pint plastic milk cartons with the bottom cut off make useful little cloches for young seedlings.

Outdoor plants will benefit from the use of a black plastic mulch which will keep down weeds, conserve soil moisture and also help to warm the soil. Plants will tolerate short periods of drought

or flooding but not extended periods with waterlogged soil. Watering is most important during flowering and fruit set. Irregular watering at this time can lead to malformed fruits and blossom end rot. Aubergines do not normally set fruit in temperatures below about 21°C (70°F). After about four weeks stake the plants with a bamboo cane to provide support when the fruits start to swell. Pinch out the top of the plant when it is about 45cm (18in) high to encourage a good bushy growth habit.

Feed using a high potash, tomato-type fertilizer or similar organic feed or comfrey liquid at weekly intervals once the first fruit has set. Large fruiting cultivars are unlikely to ripen more than three or four fruits per plant in temperate regions, so thinning any excess fruits set is useful to enable the plant to put its energy into swelling the first fruits. Smaller fruited cultivars such as 'Baby Rosanna' and 'Slim Jim' however can be very productive even when grown outdoors. Pick the fruits regularly to keep the plants producing more. Small fruits will have a better eating quality. Fruits are ripe when the skin appears glossy.

Tip!

Your finger and thumb or a jet of water is the best way to deal with minor infestations of aphids.

Aubergines are included with potatoes, tomatoes and peppers in crop rotations as they are in the same family and tend to attract much the same pests and diseases. Try not to grow them in ground that has been used for any crops in this group for the past three years. Flea beetles can be particularly damaging to small seedlings. Hardening off your seedlings on a bench or table 1m (3ft) or more above the ground limits the amount of attention they will receive from this pest. Growing

young seedlings under a layer of horticultural fleece for three to four weeks may also help.

Aphids, whitefly and red spider mite can all present problems to mature plants, especially when grown under cover. Keeping a close eye on your plants and dealing with pests before numbers can build up too much is important. Your finger and thumb or a jet of water are the best way to deal with minor infestations of aphids. Hang up sticky yellow traps to catch whitefly and wipe leaves regularly with a damp cloth at the first sign of red spider mite. Remove any dead petals still attached to developing fruit as these can be attacked by Botrytis moulds.

> *Tip!*
>
> Aubergines can be slow to establish and do not compete well with aggressive weeds.

Aubergines normally self-pollinate so seed set should produce plants that are identical to their parent. However, if you want to save seed and grow more than one cultivar it is wise to exclude pollinating insects to prevent accidental cross-pollination between cultivars. Cover a few flowers

Grow It Yourself

with muslin bags or empty teabags to prevent insects getting access to the blooms. Select fruits only from healthy, strongly-growing plants and allow them to mature on the plant until fully ripe when the skin loses its shine. Older varieties of aubergine may have 400 or more seeds in a single fruit, although newer cultivars are usually selected to have less seeds as the flesh is then more appealing for culinary use. Extract the seed by gently pureeing the diced flesh with water in a blender. Sieve the resulting mash, rinse the seeds and spread them to dry on a plate or sheet of paper. Dried seed should remain viable for around five years if kept in a cool, dry place.

If you want to try cross-pollinating two varieties to create a new cultivar you need to gently open the petals of a flower before it opens naturally and remove the stamens to avoid any accidental self-pollination. After a day or two the stigma should be sticky and receptive so you can then dab it with pollen from your other selected plant. Let the fruits develop and label them with the cross you have made.

Cultivars

Applegreen

Developed for growing in northern latitudes, this early fruiting plant grows to 60-90cm (24-36in). The attractive egg-shaped fruits weigh around 120g (4oz) and have a spiny calyx, thin pale green skins and a white, tender flesh.

Baby Rosanna

F1 Hybrid – Compact plants ideal for growing in pots on the patio or on the windowsill. They crop in around 75 days from transplanting, producing lovely, bitter-free mini-fruits, ideal for cooking on skewers at barbeques.

Black Beauty (plants grow up to 90cm (36in) and fruits weigh 400 - 800g (14-28oz))

Very popular cultivar plants with a bushy spreading habit. They produce a generous crop of purplish/black oval fruits that are broader at the blossom end in around 74 days. The fruits are of a high quality with a fine flavour.

Black Enorma (huge fruits of 600g (21oz))

As its name implies, this cultivar is early to crop and productive over a long season.

Black Stem (the fruits are a brilliant scarlet red when ripe)

An unusual cultivar from Uganda (called Ngilo). It has deep purplish-black stems, fuzzy leaves and lovely white flowers. In hot climates plants can get to 1.5m (5ft) tall but they will fruit as 30cm (12in) plants in the United Kingdom. The showy round fruits are around 2-6cm (1-3in) across. They have an odd taste more like green beans than aubergines and may be eaten either raw or cooked when green.

Baby Rosanna.

Bonica (produces an excellent crop of large, shiny purple fruits)

Fl Hybrid AGM (1995) – A French cultivar with compact bushy plants.

Calliope (small, egg shaped fruits 5 - 10cm (2-4in) long)

Fl Hybrid – Beautifully striped fruits of violet and cream produced on high yielding plants.

Casper (ivory coloured fruits 15cm (6in) long)

Fl Hybrid – An early fruiting cultivar. They have quite a mild flavour.

Diamond (prolific with fruits 20cm (8in) long growing in clusters)

Slender dark purple fruits with a dense, bitter-free flesh. It grows well in cool climates, maturing in around 70 days with good disease resistance.

Easter Egg (white, egg-shaped fruits a.k.a. Golden Egg/Bianca Ovale)

Produces ornamental fruits in just 60 days. They turn yellow as they mature and are best picked at the shiny white stage.

Fabina (produces a crop of medium sized fruits 15 - 20cm (6-8in) long)

Fl Hybrid – Vigorous plants whose fruits have a shiny black skin and keep well after picking.

Black Stem.

Fairy Tale (compact plants suitable for patio pots)

F1 Hybrid – They produce clusters of ornamental purple and white striped fruits with a wonderful bitter-free flavour and very few seeds.

Florida High Bush (disease and drought resistant)

Vigorous, very upright plants that produce a good crop of traditional large purple-black fruits.

Kermit (bushy, prolific and best grown in a glasshouse or polytunnel)

F1 Hybrid – Small round green and white veined fruit, similar to traditional fruits from Thailand.

Kurume (good cropper with purple fruits 25 - 30cm (10-12in) long)

A Japanese cultivar that is best for greenhouse use. It is very resistant to heat and drought.

Grow It Yourself

Listada de Gandia (reliable cropper with striped purple and white fruits)

The fruits have a very spiny calyx and thin skins so do not need peeling. The flesh has a sweet taste with little bitterness.

Louisiana Long Green (a.k.a. Green Banana, 18cm (7in) long fruits of 150g (5oz) in weight)

A late maturing cultivar with attractive banana-shaped light green fruits with creamy-green stripes at the blossom end.

Mohican (compact variety with shiny, white bulbous fruits)

F1 Hybrid AGM (1995) – Pick the fruits while they are fairly small to encourage the plant to maintain production.

Moneymaker (heavy cropping with a short growing season)

F1 Hybrid – The fruits are long and slim with a shiny, near-black skin.

Ophelia (small purple/black fruits best picked at 50g (2oz))

F1 Hybrid – An early cultivar with compact plants producing the first fruits after around 55 days.

Orlando (prolific crop of sausage-shaped deep purple 10cm (4in) long fruits)

F1 Hybrid – Short, bushy plants that are excellent for tubs. The fruits are bitter-free and make an interesting pickle if treated like gherkins.

Pingtung Long (lavender coloured fruits that are disease resistant)

A high yielding plant producing over 20 fruits that can grow to 45cm (18in) or more.

Red Egg (glossy, red, egg-shaped fruits, ideal for a patio pot)

A particularly attractive early cropping cultivar with a long season.

Rosa Bianca

A beautiful Italian heirloom with chubby ivory fruits that are variably washed with purple. Cropping from around 83 days, the fruits are well flavoured and bitter-free.

Slim Jim

Small plants growing to around 35-45cm (15-18in) with attractive violet tinged foliage and ideal for pots. They crop in 60 days from transplanting. The finger-shaped fruits, 10-15cm (4-6in) long, grow in clusters of three to five. They are tender and excellent for pickling when young.

Striped Toga

A very ornamental cultivar with small oval fruits growing to 7.5cm (3in) long, which ripen orange with dark green stripes. They have a strong flavour but are not bitter and will keep well after harvesting.

Thai Green Pea

Tall plants producing large quantities of tiny pea-like fruits with a rich exotic flavour. Do not leave them on the plant too long or they will become bitter. In Thailand they are used in stir fries and curries.

Red Egg (top)
Slim Jim (bottom)

89

Grow It Yourself

Turkish Orange (miniature orange-red fruits weighing 50g (2oz))

The fruits are eaten when green as they become bitter on ripening. In Asian cultures they are much used in stir-fries.

Violetta di Firenze (pick early for thin skins and tender flesh)

An heirloom cultivar from Italy with chubby, gently ruffled fruits which need a hot summer to give the best flavour.

Zebra (producing striped purple and white fruits around 15-20cm (6-8in) long)

F1 Hybrid – Plants start to crop in around 70 days.

Storing Your Harvest

Almagro is a form of pickled aubergine named after a town in the La Mancha area of Spain. Small aubergines are boiled in water then seeped in a dressing of olive oil, vinegar, garlic, marjoram and bay. They are sold in tins and jars and served as tapas all over Spain. Aubergines work well in other pickles and chutneys and the adventurous may like to try aubergine jam.

The small fruits of the related species *Solanum torvum*, known as the turkey berry in America, are called Terong Pipit or the sparrow eggplant in Malaysia where they are used medicinally to cure headaches and reduce blood pressure. They are a popular ingredient in Thai green curry and Malay sambal, a condiment made with hot peppers.

A craze among Chinese ladies in the 5th century was to use a black dye made from aubergines to stain their teeth. After polishing they would shine like silver. You may not fancy silver teeth but a toothpaste based on charred aubergines and sea salt is popular in Japan and is said to increase blood circulation in the gums, as well as being a good remedy for bee stings.

Salad Crops

The lettuce (*Lactuca sativa*) is an annual plant in the daisy family (*Asteraceae*). The family resemblance might perhaps not be immediately obvious but if you allow a lettuce to bolt you will see the small daisy-like flowers open in a soft yellow colour. Lettuce is native to North Africa, Asia and Europe. It has been cultivated since ancient times. In Egypt the lettuce *Lactuca sativa var. longifolia* was commonly grown. This is a long-leaved variety similar to the cos types grown today. It was closely associated with the fertility god Min and was considered an aphrodisiac as the milky sap that leaks from the stalk when you cut the lettuce was thought to resemble semen. Intriguingly, for other cultures the lettuce had a much less racy reputation. The Roman author Pliny wrote about a type of lettuce known as 'the eunuch's lettuce' that was meant to cause impotence and in the 17th century lettuce was recommended as suitable for monks and nuns to eat.

There is a great variety of lettuce available today, indeed the potager at the Château of Valmer in the Loire is planted with more than 100 different kinds. There are a number of distinct types. The cos lettuces, so called because they are thought to have originated on the Greek island of Kos, have large, long leaves and fairly open hearts. They tend to be quite hardy, resisting both cold and summer

Grow It Yourself

heat and have a good crisp texture. They are also known as Romaines as they were introduced to mainland Europe by the Romans. Butterhead types such as 'Valdor' have round heads of loosely packed, smooth, soft leaves, whereas crispheads eg. 'Sioux' have good, crisp leaves and form a tight heart. The latter type is referred to as iceberg lettuce when sold without the outer leaves. Batavia lettuces have crisp, frilly leaves but do not form tight hearts. The crunchy, nutty flavoured leaves grow upright to form a loose head. Batavias, like the cos group, have an excellent shelf life. Loose-leaf lettuces such as 'Salad Bowl' and 'Lollo Rosso' are very decorative. They do not form hearts and are often used as cut-and-come-again crops. They are slower to bolt than hearting lettuces. The so-called seaweed-leaved lettuces have deeply cut leaves that easily fall apart when the base of the stem is removed. 'Pentared' is a good example of this type with deep red crinkly leaves.

Red lettuces like 'Lollo Rosso' and 'Rouge d'Hiver' contain higher levels of the antioxidant quercetin, which is believed to have anti-inflammatory and anti-tumour properties. They can sometimes taste more bitter than green leaved cultivars and so are often served in a mixed salad rather than on their own. Red cultivars tend to have a shorter shelf life and so are less likely to be available in the supermarkets. They are though ideal for growing in the garden where their colourful leaves can be very decorative and they can be harvested as needed for maximum freshness and taste. The best coloured leaves are obtained from plants grown in full sun. Try 'Kendo', 'Marshall' or 'Rosemoor' which are cos types with tasty red leaves or 'Mottistone' with beautiful green and red mottled leaves.

Lettuces grow best in a cool season at temperatures of around 10-20°C (50-68°F). Seed germination is poor at temperatures above 25°C (77°F). Lettuce can be sown from midwinter onwards in a greenhouse, ready for planting outside in mid-March with a covering of fleece to protect against frosts. Starting seedlings off in modules allows them to be planted out without root disturbance which is also beneficial for related crops such as endives and raddichios. Plant seedlings out when they have five or six leaves into a fertile, moisture-retentive soil in an open site, or in hot summers, in light shade. Space small cultivars around 15cm (6in) apart and larger ones 30cm (12in) apart. If sowing outdoors, sow seed about 2.5-5cm (1-2in) apart and lightly cover with soil. Thin to the required spacing when seedlings have two or three true leaves. Summer sowings are best made outdoors to prevent seedlings wilting on transplanting. In hot weather water the drills before sowing to reduce soil temperatures. Cold-hardy cultivars can be sown outdoors in late summer and overwintered to provide an early crop in late spring.

Lettuces are not usually included in crop rotation schemes but should not be grown regularly in the same patch of ground or fungal diseases may build up. Keep lettuce crops free of weeds to prevent competition for water and nutrients and to prevent transfer of diseases such as mosaic virus. Like other leafy vegetables, lettuces ideally require a constant supply of water during their growth period. If time or water are limited, concentrate on giving a good watering two weeks before their intended harvest time. In dry conditions water regularly to keep the leaves succulent and prevent bitterness developing. Try to water the soil rather than the leaves to prevent mildew forming on wet foliage.

Older cultivars of cos lettuce had their leaves tied together with raffia as they grew to maintain a sweet-tasting white heart. Most people nowadays do not have the time or dedication to spend on such practices and fortunately modern cultivars tend to stay neat and erect, giving crisp, though green leaves, with little effort.

Grow It Yourself

Tip!

Lettuces are not usually included in crop rotation schemes but should not be grown regularly in the same patch of ground or fungal diseases may build up.

Avoid gluts of salad leaves by sowing a constant succession of small rows rather than a lot altogether. As a general guide wait for the first two true leaves to form on the first sowing before making the next. This usually takes around two to three weeks. Raising plants indoors in modules filled with a multipurpose compost allows you to plant out more plants as you harvest the mature crop. Most lettuces take around 10-12 weeks to mature. In summer when growth is fastest many cultivars can be harvested in about seven weeks from sowing.

Lettuces are often grown as a cut-and-come-again crop as many will resprout after they are cut and can yield two or more harvests from a single sowing. Some are harvested as a mature head and will produce a fresh crop of leaves from the cut stump whilst others are harvested as individual leaves as soon as they reach the required size. Cut-and-come-again salads are useful for intercropping between slower-growing vegetables such as sprouting broccoli or sweet corn. Colourful forms of lettuces are ideal for growing in potager gardens as they are so attractive. You can even allow a few to bolt to give striking spires of foliage for a few weeks.

You do not even need a garden to grow good crops of baby salad leaves; a hanging basket or window box is fine or you can use any large, flat container such as an unwanted tray, seed tray, old fruit punnet or shallow plastic mushroom boxes lined with perforated polythene. Fill with multipurpose compost, firm and sow evenly with a mixture of salad leaf plants. You can cover the seed lightly with compost but for most quick germinating seeds this is not really necessary as it is just like sowing mustard and cress. Keep them on an internal windowsill if there is nowhere suitable outdoors. Harvest the leaves by simply cutting with scissors above the level of the smallest new leaf so that the plants will regrow as a cut-and-come-again crop. Alternatively, sow the seed at a lighter density and cut mature leaves when the plants are at full growth, usually in about eight weeks. This technique works well with a range of salads such as lettuces, carrots, radishes, chards and stronger flavoured plants such as rocket and lovage. Many members of the cabbage family such as kale or oriental leaves like mizuna and 'Red Giant' mustard are ideal for sowing in October or November to produce tasty winter salads. Leaves harvested at the seedling stage are at their most tender and nutritious.

To add colour and interest to your salads, include a range of edible flowers such as the vivid blue borage, nasturtiums, pot marigolds, vibrant red *Salvia elegans*, chives and marjoram. If you grow chicory or radicchio, allowing one plant to flower will provide a handsome plant up to 2m (6ft) tall which gives a succession of beautiful sky blue flowers that can be used to enliven salads for many weeks.

Slugs and snails are probably the biggest pests of salad crops. Some plants seem to be less appetising to them, so if they are a particular problem you could try growing endive, kale and spring cabbage. Sadly the more tender sweeter crops are as attractive to slugs as they are to us. It is sometimes worth growing a sacrificial crop of sweet lettuce to attract the slugs away from your main plantings. Water your salad crops first thing in the morning to ensure that the soil surface is dry by nightfall; watering in the evening is the equivalent of advertising the opening of a first class restaurant for molluscs. Free-range ducks will eat a lot of slugs and snails in the garden, but unfortunately they are also rather partial to lettuce.

Flea beetles are particularly prevalent in the spring and early summer and will quickly perforate most oriental vegetables such as pak choi, so these are better sown in mid-summer to avoid the problem. Alternatively covering your crop with a layer of horticultural fleece will limit access for these and other pests such as aphids. Fleece tunnels, cold frames or cloches are useful for keeping off a variety of pests and wicker cloches can be effective at protecting individual plants from rabbits, pigeons or your free-range fowl.

Tip burn in lettuces is a condition in which the margins of the leaves go brown. It can be caused by drought or the overuse of fertilizers. Remove any dry tips, but the lettuce itself can still be eaten. Downy mildew may be a problem in damp weather. It is caused by the fungus *Bremia lactucae* and shows as pale angular patches on older leaves with white spores on the undersides. Limit its spread by increasing the spacing between

Tip!

If you want to save seed from your lettuces, leave them to flower and ripen seed.

plants. Cut off and burn affected leaves. Some cultivars including 'Avondefiance' and 'Frisby' show resistance to the disease.

If you want to save seed from your lettuces, leave them to flower and ripen seed. Allow to dry on the plant, then crush the seed head between your hands to release the seeds into a bucket. If the weather is not suitable for drying outside, cut the stems and hang upside down in an airy shed with a large paper bag tied around the head to collect the seed as it falls.

Lettuce Cultivars

Amorina (frilly, mottled red leaves)

An excellent cultivar for autumn sowing, it is resistant to mildew and slow to bolt.

Aruba (easy to crop, slow to bolt and ideal for baby leaf production)

Dark red oak shaped leaves that are thin and tender on a well-shaped plant. 'Bronze Guard' AGM is another good oak-leaf type with an upright habit.

Bergamo (plants are very slow to bolt)

Glossy vivid green frilly leaves that are crunchy and mildly sweet.

Bijou (cut-and-come-again crop and slow to bolt)

AGM – coloured, glossy red leaves with a frilly, blistered appearance.

Frillice (succulent leaves with a frilly appearance)

AGM – A loose leaf lettuce with bright green, crunchy leaves.

Little Gem (crisp, sweet hearts with a few outside leaves)

AGM – A dwarf cultivar of the cos group. The leaves are a rich green with a blistered appearance.

Lollo Rosso (ideal for potager gardens)

AGM – A well-known, medium sized, leafy lettuce. The beautiful burgundy coloured leaves have light green bases and a mild flavour.

Nymans (slow to bolt)

AGM – A medium-sized cos type lettuce with glossy red leaves that have a contrasting light green base. It shows good resistance to mildew.

Pandero (cut-and-come-again)

(top) Bassali
(middle) Enya
(bottom) Pentared

AGM – Similar to the popular 'Little Gem' but with leaves that are strongly flushed deep red. Plants are very uniform, making them ideal for decorative edgings to a flower bed. It can be sown at any time of the year for hearts.

Rouge Grenobloise (slow to bolt, cut-and-come-again)

A crisphead lettuce with broad red leaves.

Roxy

AGM – Butterhead type with gently waved leaves strongly edged in bronze. It is a good choice for growing in the open garden in summer and is slow to bolt.

Tom Thumb (bolts quickly and is best sown in succession)

It has small, tight heads produced extremely early in the season. The sweet tasting leaves are useful as baby leaves.

Valdor (a hardy lettuce resistant to grey mould)

Ideal for sowing outdoors in autumn, producing large, tight heads of dark green leaves. Protect winter crops with fleece or cloches in cold weather.

Webbs Wonderful (well flavoured leaves, slow to bolt)

A traditional favourite crisphead lettuce named after the family seed firm of Webbs in Worcestershire and grown in England since at least the mid 19th century.

Winter Density (tolerant of hot and cold temperatures and slow to bolt)

AGM – It is ideal for autumn sowing with crisp, dark green hearts and a very sweet flavour. The French cultivar 'Merveille d'Hiver' (Winter Marvel) is another reliable lettuce worth trying for winter cropping.

Other Salad Vegetables

Beetroot

Traditionally grown for their roots, which can be red, gold, white or striped, beetroot is often boiled and pickled, although grated and used raw in salads it provides a flash of colour and a great crunchy texture. Beetroot (*Beta vulgaris*) also makes a good leaf crop and was grown as a green vegetable in Roman times. It is one of the easiest of vegetables to grow and those cultivars with coloured leaves such as purple 'Bull's Blood' and burgundy-flushed 'Barbietola di Chioggia' are attractive enough for the flower border.

Carrots

Raw carrots are ideal grated for adding colour and a crisp texture to salads. Their lovely feathery foliage makes an ideal edging for flower borders or grow them between French marigolds to distract the carrot fly. Try some of the more unusual coloured cultivars such as 'Purple Dragon' or 'Crème de Lite' or the coreless 'Sweet Candle'.

Celery

Celery, *Apium graveolens*, is widely grown around the world for its edible leaf stalks, the fleshy taproot and its seeds, often used as spices. Old cultivars were grown in trenches and earthed up to produce long white petioles, but most modern cultivars are self-blanching. 'Tango' and 'Loretta' are both reliable open-pollinated cultivars, producing long sticks.

Corn Salad

Also known as lamb's lettuce, or mâche in France, corn salad (*Valerianella locusta*) is a low growing plant forming rosettes of long, spoon-shaped leaves. It is very hardy and is usually grown as a winter leaf crop from seed sown from mid-August to the end of September. Harvest by pulling the leaves as required. The small leaved cultivar 'Verte de Cambrai' from northern France has the best flavour.

Florence Fennel

Sweet or Florence fennel (*Foeniculum vulgare var. Azoricum*), sometimes called by its Italian name finocchio, is grown for its white, slightly flattened bulbs that have a refreshing aniseed taste and for the beautiful feathery foliage which is edible and much used as a garnish. Modern cultivars such as 'Orion' and 'Zefa Fino' are high yielding plants. Sow seed outdoors from May to July, harvesting from August to October.

Ice Plant

Mesembryanthemum crystal-linum has succulent leaves studded with crystal-like bladder cells, which sparkle in the sun. It makes a most attractive addition to the garden and always stimulates interest when fed to guests. Treat it as a half-hardy annual, sowing under cover in spring and planting out in a sunny spot after last frost.

Kale

Kales are particularly hardy members of the cabbage family, easy to grow and often very ornamental. Also known as borecole they are usually grown as a winter vegetable, but leaves picked when young and tender are ideal for adding taste and texture to salads. The Italian cultivar 'Nero di Toscano' has lance shaped deep green leaves. It is often called cavolo nero or black cabbage in Italy.

Pea Shoots

Pea shoots are the tender new growth of the pea plant (*Pisum sativum*). Used in Asian cuisine for years they are becoming popular in Western culture as a trendy 'new food' mixed with other green salad vegetables. Any pea variety that produces more leaves than tendrils can be used such as 'Oregon Giant' or any of the sugar-snap peas. Allow the plants to get to about 30cm (1ft) tall then pinch out the tops as required. For a more unusual salad you can use the pea tendrils themselves. The cultivars 'Markana' and 'Parsley Pea' produce particularly profuse tendrils. The flowers can also be eaten but you will not get a crop of peas to follow.

Radishes

Ideal for children to grow, radishes germinate quickly and crop reliably. They are related to mustard and have a similar pungent taste. There is a huge range of different root forms and colours, from globes such as 'Wintella' through to the long carrot like mooli radishes popular in the Far East. They can also be used as a leaf crop and varieties of the *Caudatus* Group such as 'München Bier' (often sold as 'Rat's Tail') are prized for their edible seed pods, although any cultivar can be used in this way with the mooli type producing particularly succulent pods.

Rocket

Eruca sativa is native to the Mediterranean area where it grows on dry disturbed soils. The leaves have a rich peppery taste and the pretty buff-coloured flowers and young seed pods can also be eaten. The wild form has the spiciest taste, but Turkish rocket is more resistant to flea beetle. Rocket is very easy to grow, maturing in around six weeks.

Spinach

Spinach (*Spinacia oleracea*) is a fast-growing annual plant with deep green, highly nutritious leaves. Mature leaves are usually eaten lightly cooked but when cut young they are delicious raw in salads. Sow seed directly where you want it to grow in spring or late summer into autumn. Spinach does not usually germinate in the heat of the summer.

Spring Onions

Salad onions are easily grown by sowing in drills from March onwards for summer crops or, for pulling in spring, sow in September. The traditional favourite is 'White Lisbon', a quick maturing, mildly flavoured cultivar. The Japanese cultivar 'Shimonita' has a sweet-tasting bulb but pungent leaves. Like the cultivar 'Long White Koshigaya' it is derived from the species Allium fistulosum, which usually produces upright, very straight onions unlike those of the traditional A. cepa cultivars. 'Apache' has very attractive deep purplish-red skins.

Grow It Yourself

Swiss Chard

You can grow watercress from a bunch bought in the supermarket.

As attractive as many more traditional ornamental plants, Swiss chard (*Beta vulgaris Cicla* group) is available in a rainbow of colours with the midribs of the leaves looking particularly vibrant in low sunlight. It is easy to grow in a wide range of soils and is excellent for tubs or windowboxes. Leaves are usually ready for harvesting in 8-12 weeks from sowing.

Tree Spinach

Chenopodium giganteum, the Mexican tree spinach, is an annual plant that reaches a height of up to 2m (6ft). The stunning leaves have vivid magenta centres and can be used young in salads or cooked like spinach when mature. The plants contain oxalic acid and should not be eaten in large quantities.

Watercress

Contrary to popular belief watercress (*Nasturtium officinale*) does not need a stream or even waterlogged soil in which to grow but will grow happily in pots of any reasonable moist compost in partial shade, producing a good harvest of peppery tasting leaves. In warm weather stand the pots in a saucer of water. Root cuttings from a bunch bought in the super-market in a glass of water on the windowsill or grow cultivars such as 'Aqua' from seed. Watercress makes a useful cut-and-come-again crop, best sown in spring or autumn as it may run to seed in high summer temperatures.

Tomatillos, Cape Gooseberries and Related Plants

The best known edible members of the *Solanaceae* family are of course potatoes, tomatoes, aubergines and peppers, but it pays to be cautious as parts of many plants in the family (as with the fruits of potatoes) can be toxic. Some members of the family are not widely grown in the United Kingdom and the easiest way to obtain seed is often by buying a fruit in the supermarket and extracting the seeds yourself. Importing the seed of *Solanaceae* plants from non-EC countries requires a phytosanitary certificate. Contact the Department for the Environment, Food and Rural Affairs (Defra) for up-to-date details. The import of the seed of potatoes and other stolon-forming species from outside the EC is prohibited.

Tomatillo

The tomatillo or husk tomato (*Physalis philadelphica*) is an essential component of Mexican cooking and has been used as food for at least 3,000 years. The fruit is tomato-like but comes in a papery case similar to that of the more familiar Cape gooseberry (*P. peruviana*). As the fruit

Tip!

Harvest tomatillos before they are fully ripe, when the husk starts to turn brown but the fruit is still green.

develops, however, it fills the husk and by harvest time has split it open and looks like someone trying to fit into a rather too tight garment. The fruits are variable and can ripen to light green, yellow or purple. They are usually harvested before they are fully ripe, when the husk starts to turn brown but the fruit is still green. At this stage they will have the fresh, tangy, grassy flavour which is greatly prized as a contrast to the hot chilli taste of much Mexican food. If left too long the fruits can become dry and mealy. Remove the husk before using the fruit and wash them to remove the natural sticky coating they have.

Tomatillos can be used fresh in salads and sandwiches and are indispensable for the Mexican green sauce, salsa verde, which can be prepared with raw or cooked tomatillos, although the best emerald colour comes from using them raw. They are also used to add flavour to stews and sauces for tacos and enchiladas. Jams and other preserves made from tomatillos are popular in Central and South American countries. Tomatillos keep for at least a couple of weeks in their husks and can also be frozen successfully either whole or sliced.

The tomatillo is an annual plant, usually growing to around 60cm (2ft). Sow the seed in mid to late spring in pots of normal seed compost kept in a warm place such as a sunny windowsill or airing cupboard. Seed usually germinates readily, within a week or two. Grow plants on and plant outside when all danger of frost is past. They will grow successfully in any reasonably fertile soil in sun or part shade or can be grown in containers or grow bags. Plants tend to sprawl and may need some support with canes and string to keep them upright and make harvesting easier. They can be grown over a net supported with stakes so that the fruits hang down and are easy to pick. In poor summers a better harvest will be obtained from fruits grown under cover.

All tomatillo flowers are hermaphrodite, that is they have both male (stamens) and female (pistils) reproductive systems. However they will not self-pollinate, so you need to grow two or more plants to get fruit set. Tomatillos often naturally drop from the plant when mature and can be gathered and used or left to ripen fully. If however the calyx drops off with no fruit formed inside, it is usually due to insufficient pollination, either because an isolated plant has not been cross-pollinated or due to a lack of bees. Containerised plants that have been allowed to dry out may also drop their fruit early. Plants are generally so productive that you would only need two to provide enough tomatillos for the average family. Most cultivars are ready to crop in around 70-75 days from planting out.

Despite the fact that tomatillos have been cultivated for thousands of years there are very few named cultivars and seed is usually sold as tomatillo - green or tomatillo - purple. Verde is the Spanish word for green and 'Toma Verde' is a classic round green tomatillo about the size of a golf ball. The similar 'Verde Puebla' may have rather larger fruits but those of the productive cultivar 'Cisineros' are probably larger than any other cultivars. 'Cisineros' has apple-green fruits which will eventually ripen to a yellowish-green. They are usually eaten at the bright green stage when they have a fresh, tart flavour. The purple forms of tomatillo are sweeter than the green and good to eat straight off the plant. 'De Milpa' is an attractive cultivar with purple stripes on the husks. It is particularly vigorous and can produce some 300 fruits per plant. The word milpa is a Mexican Spanish term meaning field, and this form of tomatillo is often found as a weed in Mexican cornfields.

The closely related plant *P. alkekengi* is a hardy perennial grown for the ornamental effect of the calyces, which turn bright orange and are known as Chinese lanterns. They can be successfully dried for indoor decorations. The fruits are bitter and should not be eaten.

Cape Gooseberry

Cape gooseberries (*Physalis peruviana*) are also known as ground cherries, golden berries or sometimes just physalis. They are native to South America but were widely cultivated in the Cape of Good Hope region of South Africa in the 1800s, hence the common name. The big bushy plants can be as much as 2m (6ft) high but are more usually about half that and tend to sprawl. They have large downy leaves and yellowish bell-shaped flowers with dark, purplish-brown spots in the throat. After fertilisation of the flower the calyx expands, forming a paper-like husk much bigger than the berry it encloses. The husk acts as a protective case for the berry which will remain in good condition for a month or more at room temperature. The fruits have an interesting sweet-sour flavour. They are usually eaten raw straight from their cases and are sometimes used in restaurants as an unusual garnish for desserts. The husk makes a perfect handle to use when dipping the fruit in melted chocolate. The fruits are a rich source of vitamins A and C and can be used in exotic fruit salads or to make excellent purées and jams. They are wonderful cooked with ginger. In Peru where the fruit is known as aguaymanto, it is used in marmalades. Dried berries can be used as a substitute for raisins. The husks are said to be toxic and should not be eaten.

The plants are easily grown from seed, which usually germinates within a week. Grow on in a frost-free place and either plant out in the garden or grow in large pots or tubs. Treat the plants much like you would a bush variety of tomato. Taller cultivars may need support with a couple of bamboo canes. Plants thrive on neglect and if overfed will produce more leaves than fruit. They do however need regular watering for the best fruit set. Whilst plants will produce fruit happily outdoors, the fruits ripen quicker when grown in a greenhouse or polytunnel. As the fruits ripen they will drop from the bush but

will continue to mature, changing from green to the rich golden-yellow of the mature fruit. Fruits will continue to form until late in the autumn. In all but the coldest areas plants cut down to about 15cm (6in) in late autumn will resprout the following spring, particularly if they are given a deep mulch.

Cape gooseberries usually grow to around 1m (3ft) tall. 'Little Lanterns' is a more compact cultivar, growing to about 50cm (20in). 'Pineapple' is a prolific cropping dwarf form. 'Giant' has particularly well-flavoured, large berries but requires a longer growing season. The old cultivar 'Aunt Molly's Ground Cherry' is a selection of *P. pruinosa*

Tip!

Whilst plants will produce fruit happily outdoors, the fruits ripen quicker when grown in a greenhouse or polytunnel.

from eastern North America. Ground cherries were grown in Pennsyl-vania as early as 1837. It is a good compact plant growing to around 45cm (18in). 'Long Ashton' was selected at the Long Ashton Research station near Bristol where the blackcurrant drink Ribena was developed.

Garden Huckleberry

The garden huckleberry, *Solanum melanocerasum*, must be one of the easiest of all fruits to grow. Plants grown from seed sown on a windowsill in early spring will start to crop within four months, producing clusters of shiny black fruit over an extended period on short, rather lanky plants. They will grow in virtually any soil, in sun or part-shade and are fairly drought tolerant. It has to be said that the fruits are not the most appe-tising of berries, bearing a close resemblance to those of their cousin the wild black nightshade (*S. nigrum*) and indeed should not be eaten green. Eaten raw they can have a fairly bland taste, although this improves if the fruits are exposed to a frost. When stewed with sugar they are much more palatable and are excellent if mixed with apples for pie making. They can be used to make a wonderful rich purple coloured ice cream.

The similar sunberry (*S. x burbankii*) is a hybrid created by the American plant breeder Luther Burbank, best known for his Shasta daisies. He said that it was a result of crossing *S. villosum* and *S. guineense*, although this has sometimes been disputed by people who think it is a simple variant of the garden huckleberry. It was introduced in the United States by the Lewis Child nursery as the 'wonderberry' but never really found favour, although it is equally easy to grow and gives sweeter berries that have a superior flavour. 'Mrs Bee's Non-Bitter' is a cultivar with sweet purple fruit that has a much better flavour than the ordinary garden huckleberry and can be eaten fresh or cooked. It is just as easy to grow as the other forms. The true huckleberry of 'Huckleberry Finn' fame is an unrelated plant, *Gaylussacia baccata*, which is a relative of the blueberry.

Goji Berries

The goji berry, *Lycium barbarum*, has attracted much media attention through being named as one of the so-called super fruits which are rich in antioxidants. They hit the news again when some stocks were found to have been illegally imported into the United Kingdom. All *Solanaceae* plants are banned from import into the EU from countries outside Europe and the Mediterranean area as they can act as hosts for some pests and diseases including viruses that could adversely affect commercial potato and tomato crops. There are however no restrictions on the berries themselves or on seed, so if you want to try growing the plants, raise them from seed. A couple of dried berries obtained from a health food store will contain plenty of seed which germinates readily after just a few days.

Young plants are best kept in a cold frame for their first winter or covered with a layer of fleece during cold spells, but as they mature they will make perfectly hardy shrubby plants that should be able to tolerate temperatures down to -15°C (5°F). They will grow happily in most well-drained soils and can be planted in sun or partial shade. They are ideal for planting as a fruiting hedge or make attractive container plants for the patio. Plants start to flower after two years, producing pretty white and purple trumpets. The fruits set in the autumn and turn a glossy red when ripe. Plants can sometimes be invasive.

Naranjilla

For those who like more of a challenge, the naranjilla is an interesting plant well worth trying. The name naranjilla comes from the Spanish for 'little orange', a reference to the round, golden-yellow fruits which have a tangy, somewhat citrusy flavour. The botanic name is *Solanum quitoense*, which means 'nightshade from Quito' as this perennial plant comes from the area around Quito in Ecuador. Plants are very ornamental with large attractive leaves that are covered in short, purple hairs and sometimes thorns. The buds of the large, fragrant flowers are also coated in purple hairs. The fruits range from golf ball size to that of an orange. They have a coating of brown hairs which can easily be rubbed off when ripe, revealing a bright orange leathery skin. A very juicy, green, jelly-like pulp

Pepino

is studded with lots of pale seeds within four seed compartments.

Seedlings are raised as you would tomatoes. Growth is rapid if they are well watered and fed, but they can be tricky to keep going and I have always lost mine before they get to the fruiting stage. Young plants can be grown in pots on the patio, although they tend to get easily battered by wind and rain and so would usually do better if grown in a polytunnel. In the greenhouse or conservatory they will need shading in hot summers. In tropical countries fruiting begins in 10-12 months from seed and plants will be productive for perhaps four years before vigour declines.

Pepino

Solanum muricatum, the pepino or melon pear, is a small bushy perennial with a woody base that usually grows to about 1m (3ft) tall, making it ideal for container growing on a patio. The leaves are very variable and may be simple ovals, lobed or divided into several leaflets. Flowers can be purplish or attractively striped in white and purple. A single plant will set fruit on its own, although fruit set is said to improve if you grow more than one clone. The fruits are quite variable although generally they are the size and shape of a goose egg, with a yellowish skin streaked in purple. The flesh is reasonably sweet, juicy and refreshing, somewhat like a melon.

Tip!

Allow the fruits to fully ripen on the plant for the maximum sweetness and flavour.

Plants are usually grown from seed as they develop quickly and will start to fruit within six months, however many different cultivars are grown commercially in New Zealand and Chile where they are generally propagated from stem cuttings. They are easy to grow in a sunny, sheltered position. Water regularly and feed once a fortnight or so with a tomato-type fertilizer. Allow the fruits to fully ripen on the plant for the maximum sweetness and flavour. They are quite delicate, so need careful handling to prevent bruising. Plants are sensitive to frost and so if you want to keep them over winter they need to be moved inside in the autumn, although plants in a well-drained, sheltered spot may survive over winter, particularly if given a deep mulch. The main problem that I have found is that the fruits are irresistible to our local rodent population.

Tree Tomatoes

If you have a greenhouse or conservatory that is maintained frost-free over the winter months you could try growing a tree tomato, *Solanum betaceum* (*Cyphomandra betacea*). It produces succulent plum-shaped fruits around 7.5cm (3in) long, which ripen to red, orange or yellow. The red forms have dramatically dark seeds. They have a tangy taste, somewhat like a passion fruit with the yellow fruits being rather milder. Fruits can be halved and the flesh scooped out as you would a kiwi or you can remove the skin and slice the fruit to eat them raw in salads. The skin and the flesh immediately under it has an unpleasant bitter taste.

Seed sown in early spring germinates in two to four weeks on a windowsill and grows on quickly. Pot seedlings individually into 10cm (4in) pots once they have their first true leaves, potting on again or planting out when they reach around 15cm (6in) in height. Alternatively propagate from softwood cuttings which root easily in a free draining compost. Grow plants in containers at least 35cm (14in) in diameter or in a bed of fertile loam soil. When plants reach around 1m (39in), pinch out the growing point to encourage a bushy shape. Plants will need to be protected from cold through their first winter and then may start to fruit in their second summer. Mature plants are hardy to just below freezing but they will fruit better if temperatures remain above 10°C (50°F) and are most productive at temperatures of 20-28°C (68-82°F). Water well during dry periods and apply a liquid tomato type feed every 3-4 weeks. Plants in pots should spend the summer outdoors to reduce attacks by glasshouse spider mites. A mature tree can produce in excess of 50kg (110lb) of fruit each year. They are not long-lived plants and the life of a commercial plantation is around just eight years.

The species *Solanum corymbiflora* (*Cyphomandra corymbiflora*) is hardier and will remain evergreen throughout the winter, tolerating several degrees of frost if kept reasonably dry at the roots. The small fruits have a pleasant taste but contain a lot of seeds so they tend not to be very popular. *Solanum diploconos* (*Cyphomandra fragrans*) from Brazil has very large glossy, evergreen leaves which have a pungent smell when rubbed. If protected from hard frosts it will grow to be a small tree of around 2m (6ft) in height, producing yellow-orange fruit that has a fuzzy coating when young. Mature fruits have quite a sweet taste. Plants of most species of tree tomato are not usually self-fertile so you would need at least two to cross-pollinate.

Perennial Vegetables

If sowing seed or buying in young plants each year just seems on occasion to be too much trouble, there is a range of vegetables that you can grow that can be left in the ground and will produce a crop for year after year. Once established many perennial crops produce vigorous spring growth which can outgrow weeds and will even be strong enough to resist attacks by slugs and other garden pests. A number of perennial vegetables will crop early in the year before annual crops are ready to be harvested, allowing you to have a productive garden over a much longer season. Several in this group of plants, such as globe artichokes and asparagus, are ornamental plants, attractive enough to be included amongst the flowers in a border in a cottage style garden.

Asparagus

Asparagus (*Asparagus officinalis ssp. officinalis*) comes from southern Europe and was introduced to Britain in the sixteenth century. It grows wild on light sandy soils. The airy fern-like foliage in summer is very pleasing and makes an excellent backdrop to colourful summer plants such as dahlias and cosmos.

Most modern cultivars such as 'Theilim'

and 'Gijulim' are all-male F1 plants which form more vigorous plants than the traditional, open-pollinated cultivars and have the added advantage that they will not self-seed around your garden. Once established asparagus crowns can crop for up to 20 years with each crown producing around a dozen spears each season. White asparagus, generally found tinned, has a more delicate flavour and tender texture. It is produced by blanching the stems by covering them to exclude the light. This can be done using an upturned bucket and inhibits the development of the green pigment chlorophyll, creating the distinctive white colouring. Recently several purple and reddish cultivars such as 'Pacific Purple' have become popular. They generally produce thinner spears that have a particularly good, sweet flavour and are ideal for eating raw. Steaming rather than boiling the purple cultivars will help to retain their colour.

Asparagus can be raised easily from seed sown in modules in late winter or early spring and transplanted in early June. Choose seeds of an all-male F1 hybrid for optimum results and sow singly to reduce root damage on potting up. Alternatively buy one year old crowns which are young dormant plants in early spring. Fork over the soil in your chosen asparagus bed and dig a trench 30cm (12in) wide and 20cm (8in) deep. Work in well-rotted manure or compost to the bottom, return around 5cm (2in) of the excavated soil and make a 10cm-high (4in) ridge down the centre of the trench. Place the crowns on top of the ridge, spacing them 30-45cm (12-18in) apart. Spread the roots evenly then fill in the trench, leaving the bud tips just visible. Water in well to settle the soil around the roots. On well-drained soil you will probably not need to worry too much about the ridge planting system. If you just want a few asparagus plants they can be grown successfully in tubs or plastic buckets with holes in the bottom for drainage. Allow one crown for a 12-15 litre (3 gallon) bucket.

An established asparagus bed requires little maintenance but should be kept weed free to prevent competition for water and nutrients, preferably weeding by hand as it is easy to damage the shallow roots when hoeing. Mulch well with a thick layer of well-rotted manure or other organic material to discourage weeds and to help retain moisture in the soil. To promote vigour a general fertiliser can be applied at a rate of around 100g per sq m (3oz per sq yd) in early spring and again after harvest. In windy areas construct a cage of canes and twine to provide support for the top-growth, preventing it from breaking off. The foliage should be allowed to turn yellow in the autumn before cutting it down to around 2.5cm (1in). Any plants bearing orange-red berries will be females which do not produce such good spears and are best removed.

Tip!

An established asparagus bed requires little maintenance but should be kept weed free to prevent competition for water and nutrients.

Do not harvest any spears in the year after planting to allow the plant to build up a good crown. Experts often recommend leaving the plants until the third year before harvesting but I suspect that not many gardeners will be able to resist that long. For the first year of harvest pick spears emerging from mid-April for six weeks and then allow the next flush of spears to develop. In subsequent years you can harvest for eight weeks. To harvest, cut individual spears every two to three days using a sharp knife. Special asparagus knives are available which have long, curved, serrated blades. Cut 2.5cm (1in) below the soil when the spears are no more than 18cm (7in) tall. Use the asparagus within a day or two of harvest for the best flavour and vitamin content. Store in the refrigerator with the ends wrapped in a damp paper towel.

Globe Artichokes

The globe artichoke (*Cynara scolymus*) is a very impressive, architectural plant with decorative silvery-green leaves and tall stems that bear the attractive purple thistle-like flowers. They usually grow to around 1.2-1.5m (4-5ft) tall with a spread of 90cm (3ft). They make superb decorative plants for the border or gravel garden but are usually grown in the vegetable garden for the green and purple flower buds which have edible, fleshy pads at the bottom of the bud scales. The base of the flower, called the heart, is also edible but the mass of immature flowers in the centre of the bud, known as the choke, is not edible. Any flowers left to open on the plant are extremely welcome to bees and butterflies.

Globe artichokes are thought to have originated in North Africa and have been cultivated for at least two thousand years. They were introduced to

Grow It Yourself

England by the Dutch and were grown in Henry VIII's garden at Newhall in 1530. Introduced to the United States in the 19th century, production there now centres on California where the town of Castroville has held an annual artichoke festival for more than 50 years.

Globe artichokes grow best in cool climates, avoiding extremes of temperature. They will tolerate some frost but may be killed in very hard winters. They prefer an open but not windy site and a fertile, well-drained soil. Plant young plants in spring about 75cm (30in) apart. Plants can be raised from seed, although the quality may vary. Seed can be sown indoors in February or outdoors from March onwards. Named cultivars are generally propagated by division. Lift established plants in spring and divide with a spade or with two hand forks. Each division should have a couple of strong shoots and some robust roots. Keep plants free of weeds and mulch to keep the soil moist in summer. In areas prone to hard frosts protect the crowns of the plants with a thick layer of straw over the winter. Healthy plants should remain productive for up to ten years, although commercially plants are replaced every three years to maintain vigour and cropping levels.

Harvest the buds when they feel plump but before the scales start to open. Cut the main bud, known as the king head, from each stem first. This allows the development of side shoots, which will produce a secondary crop of smaller, cricket ball-sized buds. If picked when small the buds do not have a choke. The flower heads are cut with about 2.5cm (1in) of stem, but this length of stem is removed before cooking to allow the artichoke to sit flat on the plate. Use promptly after harvest for the best texture and flavour, although they can be kept cool and dark for up to two weeks if necessary. The leaves may also be used as a vegetable if blanched.

The old cultivar 'Green Globe' is available as a seed strain. It is probably the most widely grown of all cultivars both commercially and in gardens. The French cultivar 'Gros Vert de Laon', named for the city in Picardy, has particularly large flower heads and good resistance to cold. 'Violetta di Chioggia', widely grown in the Venice region of Italy, is very orna-mental and richly flavoured. 'Emerald' shows greater cold-tolerance and so is better for northern gardens. 'Concerto' (F1) is a vigorous and deco-rative purple-headed variety which may well produce flower heads in the first year. Newer seed cultivars such as 'Imperial Star' and 'Northern Star' have been bred for early cropping and greater hardiness.

Some cultivars such as the Sardinian 'Spinoso Sardo' have spiny thorns on the bud scales. To make these easier to handle cut away the top quarter of the scales with scissors before cooking.

Cardoon

Closely related to the globe artichoke, the cardoon (*Cynara cardunculus*) can grow to 2m (6ft) in height. The buds are edible but best picked young before the spines develop. It is usually grown for the blanched stems which look rather like deformed celery stalks and in Italy are nicknamed gobbi or hunchbacks. The stems are blanched by gathering together the leaves from late summer to winter and wrapping them in sheets of cardboard or black plastic for 2-3 weeks to exclude the light. In the warm weather of late spring and summer cardoons become unpalatably bitter, so they are better considered a winter vegetable. They are then boiled, baked or braised until tender. Cardoons are popular in northern Italy as antipasto. If gathered young and stripped of their rind and fibres, the stalks may also be eaten raw with oil and vinegar as an accompani-ment to cold meats.

Cardoons are grown in the same way as globe artichokes but will require rather more space. Do not allow them to set seed in the garden unless all your neighbours want to grow some. Try to obtain spineless plants such as the French 'Plein Blanc Inerme'; the word inerme, unarmed, indicates that you are less likely to prick yourself on the spines.

Sea Kale

The native sea kale (*Crambe maritima*), a member of the cabbage family, was a very popular vegetable in the 19th century. Cartloads of roots were collected from the seashores for forcing in winter to provide fresh shoots, which were a delicacy for the table. Local people would also force shoots in situ by heaping seaweed or shingle over the plants to produce long, blanched stems. Cultivated forms such as 'Lily White' produce whiter stems than the wild plant. Plant divisions, known as thongs, are sometimes available from specialist suppliers, otherwise plants can be grown from seed. The seeds have a corky outer layer which enables them to float at sea for several years. Germination therefore can be very slow, so the corky case is sometimes carefully removed to speed up germination. Sow the seeds in modules or in a nursery bed, transplanting the young plants 45-60cm (18-24in) apart in their final position.

Sea kale grows best in a sandy, sharply drained soil, as at its seaside home. Leaves may be damaged by pigeons or slugs and snails but otherwise plants tend to be trouble free. Plants will take around two years to establish and then should be strong enough to allow shoots to be forced using a bucket or a rhubarb forcer. Cover the crowns in late winter and harvest the blanched shoots when they are around 20cm (8in) tall, which can take several weeks. For commercial production sea kale is lifted and potted up in November and sprouted in dark barns. It is harvested from mid-January until the end of March.

After harvest allow the normal development of further leaves to replenish the plants' strength. The leaves are quite attractive with crinkled edges and a bluish-grey succulent look to them. Stems growing up to 60cm (2ft) tall bear fluffy white flowers which are attractive to bees. The plants are not self-fertile so you will need two genetically different plants in order to get seed set.

Jerusalem Artichokes

Despite its common name, the Jerusalem artichoke (*Helianthus tuberosus*) does not come from Jerusalem and is not related to the globe artichoke. It is actually a relative of the sunflower, originating in the eastern states of North America. It arrived in Europe in the 17th century and was known as girasole in Italy, from the Italian word for sunflower. It is thought that the Italian girasole was corrupted to Jerusalem by the English. The artichoke connection is probably

the result of the explorer Samuel de Champlain, who founded Quebec City, sending some tubers to his native France with the comment that the taste resembled that of the artichoke.

The plant is tall and leggy with smaller leaves and flowers than those of the annual sunflower. It produces underground tubers that look like a cross between a ginger root and a potato. In the ordinary wild type they vary from around the size of a hen's egg to large branching tubers which can be quite knobbly. They are quite brittle with a crisp texture similar to that of the water chestnut. The colour can vary from beige or brown, through white to shades of red and purple. The cultivar 'Fuseau' has long, smooth tubers that are uniform in shape and easier to clean. 'Clearwater' from Maine in the New England region of America has the mildest taste. The Austrian cultivar 'Waldspinel' has small bumpy tubers and is one of the better coloured red varieties. The name translates as 'Gem of the forest'.

Jerusalem artichokes are probably the easiest of all vegetables to grow. All you need to do is to plant some tubers in the ground in late winter or spring and stand back to watch them grow. For preference plant 10-15cm (4-6in) deep and about 30cm (12in) apart. They are not fussy about soil type, tolerating even a heavy clay soil, and are extremely hardy. The plants are extremely vigorous and will compete strongly with weeds. In rich soil plants can grow as much as 3m (10ft) tall, so in windy areas it may be worth earthing up the stems to improve stability. Alternatively, towards the end of the summer cut the stems down to around 1.5m (5ft) so that the plants do not get rocked by wind. The tuber production is not noticeably set back by this. In very dry conditions they may benefit from additional water. Cut the foliage down to ground level as it starts to yellow in the autumn.

Tubers can be harvested as required from autumn right through the winter. If Jerusalem artichokes are not wanted in the same place for the next year, care must be taken to remove every small tuber, otherwise they can become invasive. In fact they are probably best grown in any spare pieces of rough ground where they can hold their own against nettles and other weeds and they are often used as a windbreak to protect more delicate crops.

Chinese Artichokes

Not related to globe or Jerusalem artichokes but a member of the sage family, the Chinese artichoke (*Stachys affinis*) is actually more closely related to the popular ground cover plant lamb's ears (*Stachys byzantina*), grown for its beautiful silvery, furry foliage. Chinese artichokes are grown for their small knobbly tubers which in their native China and Japan are often pickled. In France they are known as crosnes after Crosnes, a suburb of Paris that was home to Monsieur Pailleux who introduced the vegetable into Europe from the Far East in 1882.

The tubers are planted in early spring in any rich soil. Space them about 15cm (6in) apart and plant 7.5cm (3in) deep. They will grow in sun or partial shade and require very little care but prefer moist soils and in the wild will grow in wet or submersed land. Plants grow to about 45cm (18in) tall. They rarely flower or set seed in the United Kingdom. Lift the new tubers in autumn or winter once the top growth has died back. As with Jerusalem artichokes they keep fresh better in the soil and, like the aforementioned plants they may regrow from any tubers left in the ground.

Rhubarb

Rhubarb is technically a vegetable although it is eaten more often as a fruit, being valued especially when used in pies, crumbles and fools. It is a very useful plant because it can be harvested at a time when few other crops are available. It is particularly easy to grow and the large leaves tend to shade out all but the most robust weeds. Individual plants can last 20 years or more.

All species in the genus *Rheum* have edible stems but the more ornamental ones tend to be tough and stringy. Culinary rhubarb (*Rheum x hybridum*) has succulent stems which are especially tender when forced in the dark. The technique of rhubarb forcing was discovered accidently at the Chelsea Physic Garden in London. A ditch had been dug and the soil mounded up, covering some rhubarb plants that were growing alongside. Some weeks later rhubarb leaves were seen growing from the top of the mound and when the plants were uncovered the stems were found to be pale, tender and tasty. This was reported in the Transactions of the Horticultural Society of London in 1817 and led to the commercial forcing of the crop.

Rhubarb grows especially well in the cooler conditions of northern England as many cultivars require lengthy periods of cold temperatures to break their winter dormancy. This, together with the local abundance of

Tip!

Plants will take around two years to establish and then should be strong enough to allow shoots to be forced using a bucket or a rhubarb forcer.

cheap coal for heating forcing sheds in the 19th century, led to production being centred in the so-called 'Rhubarb Triangle' between Wakefield, Leeds and Bradford. In its heyday there were two hundred growers in the Rhubarb Triangle and it produced 90 percent of the world's forced rhubarb. Recent years have seen a revival of interest in rhubarb and the area is still at the forefront of production with an annual food festival held in Wakefield at which tours of local forcing sheds are available.

Rhubarb is tolerant of a wide range of soils but grows best in rich but well-drained conditions. The nurseryman that I bought my first rhubarb plants from suggested that the key to good rhubarb is to remember that it is manure for the roots and custard for the shoots. It certainly grows best in a good fertile soil to which plenty of well-rotted manure or other organic matter has been added. Rhubarb is normally planted as 'sets' consisting of a fleshy rootstock with at least one bud. Sets are planted when dormant between autumn and spring. On light soils they are planted so that the buds are covered by about 2.5cm (1in) of soil, but in heavy clay soils keep the buds just above ground level to reduce the risk of rotting. Space the plants about 90cm (3ft) apart. Apply a thick organic mulch and water well until established. Do not pick stalks in the first year of planting to allow the plant to build up a good crown. An annual dressing of manure or compost will keep plants in good condition.

To increase your stock lift and divide mature plants once the leaves have died back in autumn. Rhubarb can also be raised from seed, although seedlings may not all be identical to the parent plant. Sow seed in a seedbed outdoors in spring, thinning seedlings to 15cm (6in) apart. Plant young plants out in their permanent positions in the autumn. Rhubarb is very hardy and is generally very healthy but may occasionally be damaged by slugs or snails. Crown rot, in which bacterial or fungal infections set into the base of the plant, is more likely to occur in waterlogged soil. Affected plants should be dug up and destroyed.

Perennial Vegetables

Most cultivars of rhubarb grow to around 60cm (2ft) or taller and as much as 2m (6ft) across. 'Glaskin's Perpetual' is a more compact plant. It was developed in the 1920s by John Jessie Glaskin of Brighton. It forms short plants, usually to just 30cm (1ft) in height which mature quickly and can often be cut in the first year. It contains less oxalic acid than many other cultivars and so is less tart. It is available as a seed strain. 'Timperley Early' was named after the village of Timperley in Cheshire where it was found in the 1920s. It is one of the most widely grown of all cultivars. When forced it can be ready as early as Christmas, although in the garden the season usually extends between March and the end of July. The so-called champagne varieties such as 'Early Champagne' and 'Hawkes' Champagne' have richer coloured stems and a sweeter taste. 'Crimson Wine' is a distinctive plant with handsome red-veined leaves. 'Reed's Red' has foliage that remains dark red as it unfolds and makes an attractive addition to potager type gardens. Later cropping cultivars such as 'German Wine' and 'Canada Red' are best in areas with cold winters. 'Victoria' was introduced in 1837, the year of Queen Victoria's coronation and named in her honour by Joseph Myatt, a market gardener from Deptford who had been selling rhubarb commercially since 1810, initially relying on its perceived medicinal properties as a selling point. It is a very productive cultivar with quite a late season.

In the garden rhubarb may be forced in late winter by covering the dormant crowns with a layer of straw or dry leaves, then inverting a large bucket over them or using a special forcing pot. The plant will produce tender pink stems that are usually ready for picking in 4-6 weeks. Do not force the same plants each year but alternate so that they can regain their vigour the following year.

It is important to remember that whilst the stems of rhubarb are edible the leaves contain toxic quantities of oxalic acid and must not be eaten. Indeed, even eating excessive quantities of the rhubarb stems can lead to the formation of kidney stones, which is an extremely painful condition.

Grow It Yourself

Index

Glossary

Annual | A plant that completes its lifecycle in one growing season.

Biological control | The control of pests and weeds by the use of other living organisms.

Brassica | A member of the cabbage family.

Calyx | Collective term for the green sepals of the flower that protect it in the bud stage and form a spider-like structure on top of the ripe fruit.

Cordon | A plant generally restricted to one main stem.

Crop rotation | A system in which crops are grown on different sections of a plot in a cycle to minimize build up of pests and diseases.

Cultivar | Any cultivated variety of a plant. The term is often used interchangeably with variety.

Cutworm | The larvae of various noctuirnal moths.

Cross-pollination | The transfer of pollen from the anther of a flower on one plant to the stigma of a flower on another plant.

Determinate tomato | A bushy or dwarf tomato plant.

F1 hybrid | The term stands for 'First filial generation' and refers to a cross of two pure breeding parental lines.

Fleece | Lightweight sheet of woven polypropylene.

Genus | A category in plant classification between family and species.

Hybrid | A plant resulting from a cross between two distinct parents.

Loam | A term usually used imprecisely to denote a rich soil with a balanced mix of clay, sand and humus.

Module | Individual containers used in multiples for sowing seeds.

Mulch | A material applied in a layer to the soil surface.

Nematode | A worm-like animal also called an eelworm.

Open pollinated | Seed produced from natural pollination which can result in varied plants as opposed to the uniformity of F1 hybrids, although as most tomatoes are self-fertile their offspring tend to be consistent.

Perennial | Any plant living for at least three growing seasons.

Photosynthesis | The process by which plants use sunlight to convert carbon dioxide and water into carbohydrates.

Pollen | The male sex cells produced by the stamens.

Pollination | The transfer of pollen from anthers to stigmas.

Potash | Any of several compounds containing potassium.

Side shoot | A stem that arises from the side of a main shoot.

Solanaceae | The plant family to which tomatoes and potatoes belong.

Species | A category in plant classification containing very similar individuals.

Stigma | The part of the female sex organ that receives pollen.

Truss | A compact cluster of flowers or fruits.

Variety | A grouping of plants having distinctive features that persist through successive generations.

Grow It Yourself
Useful Addresses

Association Kokopelli, Oasis. 131 Impasse des Palmiers, 30100 Alès, France
Tél: 00 33 4 66 30 64 91 | www.kokopelli-seeds.com

The Cottage Garden Society | www.thecgs.org.uk

Department for Environment, Food & Rural Affairs (Defra)
Nobel House, 17 Smith Square, London, SW1P 3JR
Tel: 020 7238 6000 | www.defra.gov.uk

Garden Organic, Ryton, Coventry, Warwickshire, CV8 3LG
Tel: 024 7630 3517 | www.gardenorganic.org.uk

The National Society of Allotment and Leisure Gardeners,
O'Dell House, Hunters Road, Corby, Northants., NN17 5JE
Tel: 01536 266576 www.nsalg.org.uk

National Vegetable Society | www.nvsuk.org.uk

Royal Horticultural Society, 80 Vincent Square, London, SW1P 2PE
Tel: 0845 260 5000 | www.rhs.org.uk

Where to Buy

D.T. Brown, Bury Road, Newmarket, CB8 7QB
Tel: 0845 3710532 | www.dtbrownseeds.co.uk

Chiltern Seeds, Bortree Stile, Ulverston, Cumbria, LA12 7PB
Tel: 01229 581137 | www.chilternseeds.co.uk

Thomas Etty Esq., Seedsman's Cottage, Puddlebridge, Horton, Ilminster,
Somerset, TA19 9RL Tel: 01460 57934 | www.thomasetty.co.uk

JungleSeeds, PO Box 45, Watlington SPDO, Oxon, OX49 5YR
Tel: 01491 614765 | www.jungleseeds.co.uk

Nickys Nursery Ltd., Fairfield Road, Broadstairs, Kent, CT10 2JU
Tel: 01843 600972 | www.nickys-nursery.co.uk

Useful Addresses

The Organic Gardening Catalogue, Riverdene Business Park, Molesey Road, Hersham, Surrey, KT12 4RG Tel: 0845 130 1304 | www.organiccatalogue.com

Plants of Distinction, Abacus House, Station Yard, Needham Market, Suffolk, IP6 8AS Tel: 01449 721720 | www.plantsofdistinction.co.uk

The Real Seed Catalogue, Brithdir Mawr Farm, Newport near Fishguard, Pembrokeshire, SA42 0QJ Tel: 01239 821107 | www.realseeds.co.uk

Seeds By Post, Woodlands Farm, Trinity Rd., Freasley, Tamworth, Staffordshire, B78 2EY Tel: 01827 251511 | www.seedsbypost.co.uk

Seeds of Italy Ltd., C3 Phoenix Industrial Estate, Rosslyn Crescent, Harrow, Middlesex, HA1 2SP Tel: 0208 427 5020 | www.seedsofitaly.com

Simpsons Seeds, The Walled Garden Nursery, Horningsham, Warminster, BA12 7NQ Tel: 01985 845004 | www.simpsonsseeds.co.uk

Suffolk Herbs, Monks Farm, Coggeshall Road, Kelvedon, Essex, CO5 9PG Tel: 01376 572456 | www.suffolkherbs.com

Thompson and Morgan, Poplar Lane, Ipswich, Suffolk, IP8 3BU Tel: 0844 2485383 | www.thompson-morgan.com

Tozer Seeds Direct, PO Box 11, Louth, LN11 0WA Tel: 0845 430 1615 | www.tozerseedsdirect.com

Edwin Tucker & Sons Ltd., Brewery Meadow, Stonepark, Ashburton, Newton Abbot, Devon, TQ13 7DG Tel: 01364 652233 | www.tucker-seeds.co.uk

Victoriana Nursery Gardens, Buck Steet, Challock, Ashford, Kent, TN25 4DG Tel: 01233 740529 | www.victoriananursery.co.uk

The Good Life Press Ltd.
The Old Pigsties, Clifton Fields
Lytham Road
Preston, PR4 0XG
01772 633444

The Good Life Press Ltd. is a family run business publishing a wide range of titles for the smallholder, 'goodlifer' and farmer. We also publish **Home Farmer,** the monthly magazine for anyone who wants to grab a slice of the good life - whether they live in the country or the city.

Other titles of Interest:

www.goodlifepress.co.uk
www.homefarmer.co.uk